ELEMENTAL CLAIMS OF THE GOSPEL

Elemental Claims of the Gospel

WALTER BRUEGGEMANN

CASCADE Books • Eugene, Oregon

ELEMENTAL CLAIMS OF THE GOSPEL

Copyright © 2024 Walter Brueggemann. All rights reserved. Except for brief quotations in critical publications or reviews, no part of this book may be reproduced in any manner without prior written permission from the publisher. Write: Permissions, Wipf and Stock Publishers, 199 W. 8th Ave., Suite 3, Eugene, OR 97401.

Cascade Books
An Imprint of Wipf and Stock Publishers
199 W. 8th Ave., Suite 3
Eugene, OR 97401

www.wipfandstock.com

PAPERBACK ISBN: 979-8-3852-1780-9
HARDCOVER ISBN: 979-8-3852-1781-6
EBOOK ISBN: 979-8-3852-1782-3

Cataloguing-in-Publication data:

Names: Brueggemann, Walter, author.

Title: Elemental claims of the gospel / Walter Brueggemann.

Description: Eugene, OR: Cascade Books, 2024. | Includes bibliographical references.

Identifiers: ISBN 979-8-3852-1780-9 (print). | ISBN 979-8-3852-1781-6 (print). | ISBN 979-8-3852-1782-3 (epub).

Subjects: LSCH: Bible. Old Testament—Criticism, interpretation, etc. | Bible—Hermeneutics.

Classification: BS1192.5 B78 2024 (print). | BS1192.5 (epub).

VERSION NUMBER 09/04/24

Contents

Preface | vii

Part One: The God to Whom Israel Answers

  1 God in the Old Testament: Character, Agent, Problem | 3
  2 YHWH: God of Violence and Otherwise | 12
  3 Class Warfare on Earth and in Heaven | 19
  4 Uncoerced Neighborliness amid Predators | 27
  5 Commanded to Holiness | 35

Part Two: The Human Self as Member and Failure

  6 The Human Self: A Member, not a Private Operator | 45
  7 Obedience: Why Obey, Whom to Obey, How to Obey | 55
  8 Sin: How Deep, How "Original," How Forgivable | 65
  9 Racism Right from Our Earliest Texts | 75

Part Three: The Riddle of Silence and Speech

  10 On Liturgical Silence | 87
  11 Divine Silence Broken in Compassion | 95
  12 Speaking Hebrew amid the Empire | 105
  13 Voiced Pain Unanswered | 114
  14 Ultimate Awe before the Lamb | 123
  15 Divine Speech via Silence | 132

Part Four: The Landscape of Jeremiah's Sojourn
—Four Studies in the Book of Jeremiah

16 The Sermon: Jeremiah 7:1–15 | 143
17 The Trial: Jeremiah 26:1–19, 24 | 146
18 The Covenant: Jeremiah 31:31–34 | 149
19 The River: Jeremiah 51:59–64 | 153
20 Back to Basics | 158

Bibliography | 173
Scripture Index | 177
Author Index | 185

Preface

THESE SEVERAL ESSAYS ARE the outcome of my old-age work. They concern themes that have long occupied my thinking, and permit me to offer something of a summary of my work. The substance and action of the Old Testament (and consequently the entire Bible) consists in the reality of God, the agency of human persons, and the interaction between them amid the larger scope of all creation. Thus the first three sections of this book concern, in turn, God, the human agent, and the riddle of communication between them.

The first section of my book is preoccupied with the character and agency of God as different from and apart from all other reality. The holiness of God lets us speak of God, all the while knowing that our best language is wholly inadequate for speech about God. There is a strong tendency among us to offer "love" as the proper characterization of God, as in "God is love." Of course there is much merit in that claim as we consider that the faithful generosity of God has no limits. But beyond "love," "holiness" calls us to recognize and affirm that there is, for the God of the Gospel, a wild otherness about God that at times comes at us as severity in judgment and even violence, and often there is silence and absence that leaves the world bereft. Of course every reading of the Bible is inescapably selective and one could readily select the evidence for God's love that excises the risky edges of the text. But such a strategy tends to domesticate God, so that God can be accommodated to our best ethical thinking. Such a strategy is congruent with neither the claim of the text nor the evidence of our lived experience.

The holy God, in the dramatic articulation of the biblical text, is ready and able to engage in vigorous dispute with alternative claimants. To be sure, organized religion and the requirements of the state cause us to tone down the wildness of God. In the end, however, the evidence in the Bible and in our lives is too strong to be censored out.

The holiness of God, moreover, is a mandate to the people of God to order their lives in terms of that holiness. Thus we are able to see that Israel worked diligently through holy times (Sabbath), holy places (sanctuaries), and holy rules concerning food, sexuality, and every aspect of lived reality to match its life to the holiness of God. Unfortunately these efforts at human holiness often took on a life of their own, wherein holiness became a mark of defensiveness or purity or exclusion that is remote from the requirements of holiness. The holiness of God is characteristically and recurringly in conflict and contestation with alternative ways to imagine divinity. As a result, alternatives to YHWH are characteristically regarded as idols, that is, as false objects of loyalty and worship, whereas YHWH insists upon being a subject of active agency and transformative effectiveness.

The counterpoint to this God, in my second section, is the human person as a partner with YHWH in the covenantal enterprise of managing creation. A gospel enunciation of human personhood contradicts the modern, rationalistic, capitalist notion of the human persons as autonomous agents. In truth human persons are characteristically and inescapably members of a community. Thus engagement with the holy God of Israel is always as a member of the community of covenant with God. We do not and cannot come to God in our autonomy, but only as a member of the community that is summoned by God's commandments and that is sustained by God's faithful promises. Thus the central feature of human life in covenant community is the question of obedience: who may issue legitimate commands to us, and who may keep life-giving promises to us? The community of faith, in Judaism and in Christian tradition, defines our emancipated selves as emancipated for a life of joyful obedience to the God who gives us life and who summons us to a neighborly existence. The relationship of the community of faith with the God who summons and sustains us is one fraught with risk. As a result of this dependence and reliance on God is that the responsibilities that come with human creatureliness are pervasive and insistent. From the outset our human enterprise has struggled with identification with and faithful participation it this relationship, often seeking lesser demands and trusting lesser promises. Thus the human side of the equation is loaded with ambiguity and irresolution.

Nowhere is this ambiguity and equivalence more evident or more costly than in our deep, ancient, and contemporary practice of racism. Since the genealogy of Noah's three sons and the judgment against Canaan, we have been wont to create a taxonomy of the human community with ranking and rating of superior and inferior (Genesis 9:18–27). It turns out that racism is the most pervasive and pernicious of all of our forms of disobedience. And the seduction of racism will surely persist long after our society has come to terms with questions of class and gender. The claim of the faith community to be "chosen" and "elect" has only provided an impetus for the claim of white superiority that is readily translated into "European-American supremacy with its long-running colonialism that has regularly issued in enslavement of "lesser" peoples and too often has culminated in genocide, all readily justified by being "chosen."

The wonder of our human predicament is that the holy God is also capable of forgiveness. In the best self-disclosures in the Bible, God is not a score-keeper, but is capable of always beginning again with new possibility. That forgiveness by God, however, is not easy and grace from God is not cheap. Thus Israel in its waywardness is summoned always again to recommit to the requirement of covenant, and so to amend conduct and policy that are counter to the will and purpose of its covenant partner. Specifically, the God of generous embrace requires redress for the long history of racist exploitation and racist violence practiced by the community in which the "unwelcome other" is treated with violence, exploitation, and finally genocide.

The wonder of this incommensurate relationship between covenant partners, between sovereign and subject, between potter and clay, is that Israel can experience lively, ongoing, and invested interaction with the holy God. Thus the "holy one" is readily characterized as "the holy one of Israel," that is, one who is passionately committed to Israel. Because the Bible is an ongoing conversation, it is no great surprise that these two incommensurate covenant partners can engage in talk with each other. Thus Israel can dare to recall the utterance of God in both narrative and poetry. In its recall, the holy one can variously speak command, promise, reprimand, and threat, all of the sorts of utterance that belong to a lively, honest relationship. Israel is unembarrassed by the claim that it has been addressed by God in ways that identify Israel and make Israel's life a counterpoint to the life of YHWH. Conversely Israel can readily recall its own speech addressed to God that consists, variously, in praise, doxology, and thanks, and petition, lament, and protest on the other hand. The outcome of such habits of speech is that we get this relationship in two very different modes. On the one hand, we get a more conventional articulation of interaction with the God who commands and promises, to whom Israel responds in praise, doxology, and thanks.

The wonder of this conventional speech, however, is that very often we have a role reversal in which Israel speaks first to address God in imperative petition, and God is left to answer, most often to respond in assurance. It is this role reversal that permits Israel to be the initiator that most desperately marks this interaction and assures that YHWH is a subject and not an object. The most important case of such an exchange is the utterance of Israel in Exodus 2:23 wherein Israel in its unbearable status as suffering slaves can break the stultifying silence imposed by Pharaoh, and cries out in need and urgency. The wonder of that history-initiating cry is that "God heard, God saw, God knew, God remembered, and God came down to rescue." This exchange that begins the Exodus narrative is a model for the ongoing conversation of Israel and God in which, given different circumstances, either party can readily take the initiative.

But of course such lively, ongoing interaction is often marked and interrupted by silence. In the third section of this book, I have probed the dialectic of speech and silence that marks this peculiar relationship. On the one hand, the God who readily addresses Israel can settle into silence. Sometimes that silence is reckoned by Israel to be absence or disregard. Sometimes it is rendered as unspeakable awe before the overwhelming majesty of God. Sometimes Israel's petition can summon the silent God back to speech and transformative action. And sometimes the silence of God is known to be so freighted that the silence itself constitutes the self-giving transformative graciousness of God. Silence can be imposed by the stronger party in order to stifle the speech and viability of the lesser party. The silence is thus as complex and problematic as is speech between the two parties.

In the fourth and final section of the book I turn yet again to the book of Jeremiah in which I have, over time, invested much of my scholarly energy. It is indeed possible to see in the book of Jeremiah the utterance of God as prophetic oracle claims to be the speech of God. And in Jeremiah's well-known laments and complaints we get bold human speech addressed to God as pathos-filled, demanding insistence. Jeremiah, moreover, knew about the silence of God. He affirms that the holy God who is close at hand is also a God "far off" (23:23), remote and inaccessible. We may imagine, as the book of Jeremiah stretches from the demise of Jerusalem to the anticipated return of exiles, that the prophet has collapsed the long years of exilic displacement as a long silence in which Israel waited, sometime in hope and sometimes in despair. The linkage between the demise of Jerusalem and the anticipated end of exile is voiced in the letter Jeremiah wrote to the exiles in Jeremiah 29. In that letter the prophet has God promise that God intends good and restoration for bereft Israel. Thus the prophetic letter proposes to fill the long years of displacement with eager expectation and longing.

In this fourth section of the book I offer four brief studies in the book of Jeremiah. These expositions concern, for the most part, quite familiar texts. The "sermon" of Jeremiah reiterates the covenantal requirements of the tradition of Deuteronomy. In that tradition Israel has no way forward except via radical repentance. Through such possible repentance, the tradition offers a return of restoration and wellbeing. The narrative of the trial of the prophet, second, articulates the contradiction between prophetic possibility and established institutional power that only wants to silence the disruption of prophetic alternative. The oracle concerning of "new covenant" offers a new historical possibility from the God of the covenant in which God will not linger longer over Israel's sin and iniquity. For good reason the church has linked "the new covenant" to the life of Jesus, even though the prophet has on horizon a more immediate social renewal. My fourth exposition concerns the sinking of Babylon in the mighty river is least well known of these Jeremiah texts. The prophet, it is reported, commits a symbolic act that means to end of Babylonian power and, consequently, the emancipation of displaced Israel. The episode features the mighty capacity of God to unseat worldly power, an inversion that was accomplished in this case through the rise of Persian power. Prophetic discourse, in this instance, has no interest in geo-political details but is preoccupied with the faithful emancipatory power of God.

In sum the prophet Jeremiah models the several elements of my book. It offers a vigorous articulation of God's holy power and purpose in the presence of God's covenant partner. It articulates, to a lesser extent the needs and hopes of Israel who must rely on the holy God for succor and restoration. It enunciates the two-sided speech of covenant, and knows about the silence of God wherein Israel, via the prophet, knows about divine absence. It is no wonder that the book of Jeremiah can be recognized as the quintessential articulation of covenant. The book is a rough and tumble account of covenant broken and covenant restored, a dramatic process that permeates the life and memory of Israel.

Preface

It remains for me to offer thanks to the usual suspects. That first of all concerns K. C. Hanson and his ready receptivity of my work for publication. It includes the patient, attentive editorial work of Tia Brueggemann. And the book reflects the generosity and support of a host of my best academic friends, many all of whom work with the book of Jeremiah. Among them are Sam Balentine, Bill Bellinger, John Bracke, Ron Clements, Ellen Davis, Terry Fretheim, Patrick Miller, Kathleen O'Connor, Carolyn Sharp, Louis Stulman, as well as my Jeremiah teachers, Lionel Whiston and James Muilenburg. We know that Jeremiah the prophet survived and was sustained by a community of support that included Baruch the scribe and the political leader, Shaphan. So for me, I am sustained by a wondrous company of generous colleagues to whom my debts are abiding.

The lively, ongoing interaction between God and God's people is a wonder for our time and place. We face the unrelenting force of predatory capitalism and the problematic gifts of technological advances that together seek to define our human possibilities. In that environment, this old testimony from the Bible sounds at best a faint echo, without force or compelling power. And yet, the old text persists. It continues to have its say, and it continues to draw to itself those who push deeper beyond modern characterizations of our existence. When King Jehoiakim burned the scroll of Jeremiah, the prophet made a new scroll and "many similar words were added to it" (Jer 36:32). So it is as the scroll keeps emerging to have its minority say. The old scroll continues to insist that God's holiness, in defiance of all of our categories, must have its say among us. I am grateful for the community of the faithful (that cuts across all our confessional lines) that continues to heed its cadences and to esteem its subversive rendering of our moment of cultural, historical reality.

Walter Brueggemann
Pentecost 2024

PART ONE

The God to Whom Israel Answers

1

God in the Old Testament

Character, Agent, Problem

THE GOD DISCLOSED IN the Old Testament—in narrative, oracle, and song—is all at once a *character*, an *agent*, and a *problem*. What follow is a reflection on the way in which the God of the Bible is a problem. This God is a problem for us in the intellectual sophistication of modern kind and in our affluence that is tilted toward self-sufficiency. We are on notice, however, that the notion that this God is a problem is not simply a modern one. It was, for many, a problem in the ancient world as well. This God is always a problem for those who find a relational, transactional practice of reality too difficult. In what follows it is necessary to consider the character of this God and the agency of this God in order to face the problem that God poses for us always, in ancient time and in our own time.

I.

It is, at the outset, important to recognize that God is recurringly embedded in narrative (that may be expressed as song). Israel's preferred way to witness to God is through story-telling. Two aspects of narrative are worth noting. First, narrative presents one-time, singular events that are described and remembered with peculiar specificity. They do not tell of repeated or routinized occurrences. They do not proceed by logical consistency, but allow room for disjunction, contradiction, reversal, hyperbole, and surprise.

There is indeed a match between *narrative mode* and the *narrative character of God*.

Second, narrative is always an artistic act of human imagination. The reality of God given us in the biblical text is necessarily rendered and mediated through the perceptual field of the human artist. This means, inevitably, that the God given us is a God humanly imagined (even if we accept the claim that it is "spirit-led" imagination). The outcome of such artistry is at times compelling, but at times disconcerting and affrontive. We must no doubt allow for a good deal of human projection, the kind we find in every artistic rendering of every reality.

The God rendered by and artistically imagined in narrative is a *character* embedded in a plot. This character with an unpronounceable, unpronounced name (YHWH) and a specific identity is recurringly part of a plot of "out of . . . into":

out of chaos into creation,

  out of barrenness into birth,

    out of slavery into freedom,

      out of hunger into food,

        out of exile into homecoming,

          out of toxic abandonment into sustaining companionship, and finally,

          out of death into life.

God, as a character in that plot is, perforce, always a character in relation to other characters, impinged upon by other lively presences, and engaged with and responsive to other characters. The *relatedness of God* as character is succinctly and perhaps normatively put in the classic self-declaration of God (also artistically rendered in human imagination:

> The LORD, the LORD,
> God merciful and gracious, slow to anger,
> and abounding in steadfast love and faithfulness,
> keeping steadfast love for the thousandth generation,
> forgiving iniquity and transgression and sin,
> yet by no means clearing the guilty,
> but visiting the iniquity of the parents on the children
> and the children's children
> to the third and fourth generation. (Exod 34:6–7)

In this recital, we are given an inventory of God's favorite modifiers: merciful, gracious, abounding in steadfast love and faithfulness. That list, however, is followed by an utterance of sternness about "visiting iniquity" for time to come. This little phrase seems to contradict the earlier part of the utterance. YHWH is said to be capable of both *gracious forgiveness* and *severe retaliation*. This double utterance portrays YHWH as having a complex and unsettled internal life that is fully capable of emotional extremity that reaches from a yearning embrace to an off-putting harshness. The narrative of Exod 32–34 (in which this recital of 34:6–7 is embedded) seems to require such emotional extremity because this God, embedded in the plot, can terminate in harshness (Exod 32:28, three thousand people!). This same God can begin again in self-giving generosity and wonder-working on behalf of Israel (Exod 34:10, a new covenant expressed in "marvels"). Such emotional extremity on the part of God results in forceful actions that strike us as logically unacceptable when stated together; they are, however, permitted and essential to the telling of the tale of *covenant broken and covenant renewed* that is a main plot line of YHWH and this people in an on-going drama of fidelity and fidelity betrayed.

Because the narrative accounts of YHWH can allow for such emotional extremity, it does not surprise us that in narrative rendering the emotional extremity of God's *interior life* and *external performance* can be pushed, in artistic imagination, even beyond the bounds of acceptable negativity. Thus we may allow, in familiar patriarchal rendering, for the judgment of God. We find it more difficult to allow for the unrestrained harshness of God in "killing enemies" (as in Josh 10:19–20, 32), or in what seem to be binges of outrage voiced by YHWH in prophetic oracle in which YHWH lashes out at YHWH's own covenant partner (as in Amos 4:6–11). The covenant itself allows for righteous indignation expressed as covenant curse and divine judgment; but some of the shrillness goes well beyond such a credible limit, as in Ezek 16:35–43).

Then we remember that we are in receipt of artistic human imagination. Such rage at betrayal was surely taken seriously in that ancient world that was shaped and conducted as a shame-based society. We may understand how such humiliation at betrayal might evoke such rage for a man in a patriarchal society when publicly betrayed and exposed as betrayed before his companions. Such rage at humiliation might be available on the horizon of the artist, as for example Hosea in his troubled marriage under a felt mandate from God (Hos 3:1 and then 2:2–13), or Jeremiah in his sad loneliness (Jer 15:5–10), or Ezekiel in his odd imagination about how a cared-for child may become the object of affection of a lustful, erotic kind (Ezek 16:4–15). We are left to decide, when we read, how or whether or in what way to receive such utterance as "divine disclosure." We are in any case on notice both: a) that this is there in the text; and b) that the portrayal of God cannot be reduced to what is comfortably acceptable to us.

This narrative rendering of God may scandalize us and we may dismiss it as human projection or as a kind of "primitivism" which is subsequently "overcome" in more acceptable narrativity. But even given such explanatory escape hatches, we are compelled to recognize that someone somewhere in our inheritance intended this seriously as "divine disclosure." On that ground it seems to me we must take the artistry seriously, live with it, engage it, regret and critique it, but not easily dismiss it from our horizon. We have in some way to live with where we have been with the God given us in the text, perhaps in repentance or perhaps more poignantly in an urging that God must repent of such conduct. Such an urging would be something of a replication of the urging of Moses that God should back off from negative propensity that occupies YHWH's character, as in Exod 32:11–13 and Num 14:13–19. We thereby recognize that we are given a character who does not easily or readily conform to our preferences. Such negative sketches of God serve to fill out the portrayal of a character who operates in freedom, who yearns for relationships, and who enters such relationships with a self-regard that is intense and sometimes self-defeating. It is clear that Israel is wholly and unabashedly committed to sketching God in relational terms that include the risks, vulnerabilities, and depths that go inescapably with personhood.

II.

In these narratives, songs, and oracles, God is a character defined in emotional extremity, an extremity that posits passionate love and profound agitation when that love is violated. More than that, however, the God given us in the text is *an agent* who can be the subject of active verbs, one who acts in causative ways, who "calls into existence the things that do not exist" (Rom 4:17). The narratives report such transformations. Thus in the exodus narrative, God delivered:

> I am the Lord, and I will free you from the burden of the Egyptians and deliver you from slavery to then. I will redeem you with

an outstretched arm and with mighty acts of judgment. I will take you as my people, and I will be your God. You shall know that I am the Lord your God, who has freed you from the burdens of the Egyptians. I will bring you into the land that I swore to give to Abraham, Isaac, and Jacob; I will give it to you for a possession. I am the Lord. (Exod 6:6–8)

We are given a series of strong verbs of emancipation, and God is subject of all of them. The narrative that follows, moreover, details the enactment of that resolve. In the narrative that follows, there are of course human agents—Moses and Aaron—who do some of the heavy lifting. There is no doubt, however, that the narrative attributes the primary action of emancipation to the resolve of YHWH.

In prophetic oracle, divine resolve comes as a series of active verbs:

> For a long time I have held my peace,
>   I have kept still and restrained myself;
> now I will cry out like a woman in labor,
>   I will gasp and pant.
> I will lay waste mountains and hills,
>   and dry up all their herbage;
> I will turn the rivers into islands,
>   and dry up the pools.
> I will lead the blind
>   by a road they do not know,
> by a path they have not known I will guide them.
>   I will turn the darkness before them into light,
>   the rough places into level ground.
> These are the things I will do,
>   and I will not forsake them. (Isa 42:14–16)

The song exhibits no embarrassment or curiosity about such a divine resolve, nor does it offer any explanation for such divine capacity. It belongs to the rhetoric of Israel, and to the God given by that rhetoric, that YHWH can be such an agent of such transformations.

In Israel's responsive doxologies, Israel has no doubt that YHWH is capable of such transformative acts. In its hymns Israel can recite the characteristic and recurring acts of YHWH:

> The Lord upholds all who are falling,
>   and raises up all who are bowed down.
> The eyes of all look to you,
>   and you give them their food in due season.

> You open your hand
>> satisfying the desire of every living thing.
> The Lord is just in all his ways,
>> and kind in all his doings.
> The Lord is near to all who call on him,
>> to all who call on him in truth.
> He fulfills the desire of all who fear him;
>> he also has heard their cry, and saves them.
> The Lord watches over all who love him,
>> but all the wicked he will destroy. (Ps 145:14–20)

> The Lord sets the prisoners free;
>> the Lord opens the eyes of the blind.
> The Lord lifts up those who are bowed down;
>> the Lord loves the righteous.
> The Lord watches over strangers;
>> he upholds the orphan and the widow,
>> but the way of the wicked he brings to ruin. (Ps 146:7b–9)

More surprising is Israel's readiness to accuse YHWH of taking unmerited negative actions against Israel, but actions nonetheless:

> Yet you have rejected us and abased us,
>> and have not gone out with our armies.
> You made us turn back from the foe,
>> and our enemies have gotten spoil.
> You have made us like sheep for slaughter,
>> and have scattered us among the nations.
> You have sold your people for a trifle,
>> demanding no high price for them,
> You have made us the taunt of our neighbors,
>> the derision and scorn of those around us. (Ps 44:9–14)

And on a more intimate, personal note:

> You have put me in the depths of the Pit,
>> in regions dark and deep.
> Your wrath lies heavy upon me,
>> and you overwhelm me with all your waves.
> You have caused my companions to shun me;
>> you have made me a thing of horror to them . . .
> Your wrath has swept over me;
>> your dread assaults destroy me.
> They surround me like a flood all day long;
>> from all sides they close in on me.

> You have caused friend and neighbor to shun me;
> my companions are in darkness. (Ps 88:6–8a, 16–18)

These texts exhibit the conviction and the verbal practice of crediting to YHWH disastrous outcomes, both public and personal.

III.

It becomes clear that Israel's artistic rendering of God fully depends upon YHWH as character and agent. Indeed, it is impossible to imagine "faith in God" in the Old Testament without this rhetoric that traces the character and agency of God in quite concrete ways. Of course it is this rhetoric concerning God as character and agent that makes the God of Israel endlessly interesting to us. We love to tell our children the more "user friendly" parts of this rendering of God.

It is, however, the same uncompromising artistry of rhetoric that presents YHWH as an *acute theological problem*. Much of the actual content of YHWH's character and agency is an affront to us and we want, as we are able, to explain away such negative dimensions of God. If we are honest, however, it is not only the extreme negativities that offend us, vexing as they are. In fact it is the entire rhetorical exercise in narrative, song, and oracle that makes this God much too particular, undomesticated, and intellectually embarrassing to us.

But then we are bound to ask:

> Too particular for whom?
>
> Too undomesticated for whom?
>
> Too intellectually embarrassing for whom?

Clearly the initial artists did not find YHWH to be so. Nor did the subsequent canon-makers find it so, for they offer such "disclosures" without comment.

But there were no doubt skeptics, cynics, and "reasonable" people in that ancient world who found this "character" and "agent" too much to bear, too much in violation of common sense. They were the ones who declared:

> He will do nothing.
> No evil shall comer upon up,
> > and we shall not see word or famine.
> > (Jer 5:12; see Zeph 1:12)

They imagined more benign, "manageable" gods, the ones taken in the Bible to be irrelevant, moribund idols (see Ps 115:4–8). We in our modern urbanity are tempted to the same dismissive reduction of God to one more to our liking and more compatible with our own autonomous way in the world. In our time that refusal of this God as character an agent is because this God is

—too particular for us in our Enlightenment rationality;

—too undomesticated us for us in our affluent control;

—too intellectually embarrassing for us in our modern world come of age.

Our intellectual assumptions are vigorously contradicted by this God, since we live in a world where we take ourselves and those like us as the only actors. We are children of Descartes and share his "turn to the subject." We cannot imagine an actor outside ourselves who may have genuine transformative capacity. And so we appeal to "better" rendering of God, whether found in doctrinal formulations that have transposed YHWH into majestic categories of perfection, or we are drawn to a more centrist moral imagination in which God conforms to our best norms. Or we settle for a God who is object rather than subject, a reduction that better accommodates our modernity with its embarrassed rejection of "an interventionist God."

In making these interpretive moves we escape the awkwardnesses of this ancient testimony, most often forgetting that such "better" renderings are also acts of artistic imagination, albeit artistic imagination that we find more congenial. We can, if we will, *eliminate the "character of God"* with emotional extremities that violate our sense of propriety. We can, as we are able, *overcome the notion of divine agency*, accepting it only in broadest, safest ways, forfending the concreteness of the narrative claims. When we engage in such convenient reductions and such respectable domestications, however, we discover—perhaps too late—that we have thereby censured what is most interesting in the tradition. Theologically we have left ourselves a God so small and thin to be not much more than a good luck charm.

But the disclosure of YHWH admits of no such taming. Because the notion of "God," taken seriously, outruns our best hopes and our deepest yearnings for one who is out beyond our horizon. Only a God capable of raging impatience may be the God able to go to the depths of sorrow with us, to the surprise of forgiveness, to the savagery of injustice well beyond. This is the God who declares,

> I form light and create darkness,
>> I make weal and create woe;
>> I the Lord do all these things. (Isa 45:7)

Alan Paton witnesses to his son concerning this God:

> He is not greater than Plato or Lincoln,
> nor superior to Shakespeare and Beethoven,
> He is their God, their powers and their gifts proceeded from him
> . . .[1]

---

1. Paton, "Meditation for a Young Boy Confirmed."

2

YHWH

God of Violence and Otherwise

YHWH, THE GOD OF the Old Testament, is featured as creator of heaven and earth, sovereign over the nations, and deliverer of Israel. YHWH is presented as a lively character and an effective agent who is embedded in the narrative of the world. YHWH is presented in intensely personal terms, vigorously engaged in practices of fidelity that require committed give and take. Being embedded in the narrative of the world, it is not surprising that YHWH's "time" (history) is characterized by all kinds of surprises, uncertainties, and contradictions. In parallel fashion YHWH's "space" (the realm ruled by YHWH) is an arena of intense dispute. That range of surprises and uncertainties evokes in YHWH a spectrum of emotional extremities, all the way from pathos-filled compassion and forgiveness to harsh responses of punishment, both in the interest of YHWH's self-regard as one who will not be mocked, and in the interest of the well-being of Israel, YHWH's chosen people. One aspect of those extreme emotive responses is a spillover into violence. That violence is not welcome among us and is not easily justified. But it is there in the text and in the character of God.

This attribution of violence to God in the Old Testament is an acute interpretive problem, both because it is in principle offensive and because it does not cohere with our shared sense of the Christian Gospel that features a God compassion, gentleness, and forgiveness. The evidence of this incongruity requires enormous theological imagination and evokes important interpretive energy. Our task is to try to understand that violence and not lightly explain it away.

I.

We may identify two areas or Old Testament texts in which the violence of YWH is especially important and especially problematic.

1. The story of the "conquest of the land of promise" is told with YHWH's authorization of violence on the part of Israel in order to secure the land (see Josh 6:1; 8:1; 10:8). While the action is undertaken by Israel under Joshua's leadership, there is no doubt that it is at the behest of YHWH. Thus while the land is *promised and given* by YHWH to Israel, it is in the end *taken* by forceful brutal military action against the indigenous Canaanite population. Thus the wondrous "land promises" of Genesis (Gen 12:1; 15:18–20; 17:8; 26:4) are transposed into tales of violent conquest. The narrative report became a foundation for subsequent vigorous claims to the land into our own day. That claim is all the more pernicious because that God-authorized assault on indigenous populations has been utilized, in the modern world, to justify colonization and conquest of indigenous populations, not least Native Americans. In such divinely authorized violence YHWH is acting out a promise of fidelity to YHWH's chosen people Israel. The violence is itself a subset of the notion of being YHWH's chosen people.

2. The second cluster of texts concerning YHWH's violence is the voicing of prophetic invective against those who do not measure up to the rule of YHWH. These "speeches of judgment" are grounded in the old covenantal curses from which YHWH enacts "sanctions" against those who violate covenantal commitments (see Deut 28 and Lev 26).

The prophetic corpus is populated with "Oracles against the Nations" in which the prophet rails violently against the nations that do not submit to YHWH's rule (See Amos 1–2; Jer 46–51). The recurring charge against the nations is that they are characteristically filled with hubris and arrogance. They imagine that they are autonomous agents who can do whatever they want without reference to the will of YHWH. In some texts the charge against the nations is more specifically related to brutality or to a lack of mercy, so that a case can be made that the nations are judged by "natural laws" of civility, decency, and justice that are intrinsic to the structure of creation (see Amos 1:3, 6, 9, 11, 13). According to the Helsinki Declaration, such acts might be seen as "crimes against humanity." Here they are "crimes against the creator."

These oracles of violence are addressed against the nations. It is surprising, however, that the primary target of this rhetoric concerns YHWH's initiative against YHWH's chosen Israel who has not, in prophetic reckoning, kept the commandments. In such a rhetorical assault on Israel, the potential for violence from YHWH is even more intense and sustained, because YHWH is not only *a disobeyed sovereign* but *a betrayed partner* sometimes imagined as a shamed husband or as a humiliated father (see Jer 3:1–5, 19–20). This cluster of "texts of violence" concerns the defense of YHWH's honor that is variously denigrated by the actions of the nations or of Israel.

3. A subset of the prophetic invective concerns Israel's recurring prayers for vengeance in the Psalms; Israel urges YHWH to take vengeance against its enemies on the assumption that the enemies of Israel are, perforce, the enemies of YHWH. Thus an Israelite can hate the enemies of YHWH "with a perfect hatred," readily identifying "my enemies" with the enemies of YHWH (Ps 139:22). The cry for vengeance in the service of justice is a human counterpoint to the divine resolve of prophetic invective that aims at the enhancement of YHWH's uncompromising rule. In its thirst for vengeance Israel seems to "imitate" YHWH's own readiness for violence. Israel becomes like the God it worships!

In these two major cluster (and one sub-set) of texts divine violence is on *behalf of YHWH's chosen* (conquest of the land) or in the *interest of YHWH's self-regard* (prophetic invective). Both motifs arise where the rule of YHWH is at risk, or where YHWH must reassert sovereign rule against rivals for sovereignty. YHWH is seduced into violence by a sense of jeopardy about the well-being of Israel or the proper honor of YHWH. It is as though YHWH acts, in the face of such challenges, out of anxiety for God's own self or for Israel's well-being.

II.

On the face of it one must recognize that such a characterization of YHWH is present in the text, front and center. Anyone who comes "innocently" to the Old Testament is sure to be surprised or scandalized by such divine performance. It is not a surprise that this witness of the text requires our attention in an effort to soften the scandal of this divine performance or to explain it away. We may identify two major interpretive strategies for this purpose, both of which have had important support over time.

1. The easy and obvious point to make is that these portrayals of God are simply *human projections* that reflect ideological passions that are "kicked upstairs" to God. As human projections these portrayals of God are not to be taken as serious theological data. Such human projections may be evoked by a radical conviction of divine commitment to Israel as God's chosen people, so that YHWH becomes a support for and function of Israel's self-understanding. One can trace that propensity in some forms of tribal/national tradition; one can, moreover, see the same propensity in the U.S. projection of "God with us" as an American god. In more recent form, discerning feminist scholars have understood that such projections of a machismo God reflect patriarchal assumptions in which God is presented as the perfect performance of virile force and power. In post-colonial interpretation, moreover, the same critique is made when the colonial power imposes its will in brutal ways as an act in obedience to the sovereign God of imperial destiny (U.S. Manifest Destiny!). All of these critiques make clear that it is not necessary or even possible to take such divine portrayals with theological seriousness. Indeed to take them in a serious way is ludicrous and irresponsible.

2. A second response to texts of divine violence of long and credible standing is the *developmental-evolutionary hypothesis* about the religion of Israel. In this hypothesis (enshrined in critical study as "The Documentary Hypothesis" of J, E, D, P), it is proposed that "Israelite religion" **evolved** (the key term!) from primitive to sophisticated, from mythic to historical, from polytheistic to monotheistic, and from cultic to ethical. The hypothesis has had long credibility because is serves to explain a great deal in the text.

It is, however, widely recognized that such a hypothesis contains at its core an embrace of "supersessionism," a notion that "better" articulations of faith **supersede** (the key word!) what has come before, so that the earlier and more objectionable, embarrassing parts of the testimony may be scuttled and disregarded in order to focus on the more recent that is easily judged to be "superior."

The supersessionist denial of divine violence (as human understanding evolved) is problematic on two counts. First, the hypothesis has Christian origins with a tacit claim (in the nineteenth century) that the "evolution" of God continued in order to arrive at Christianity (and with it the superiority of Western Christian culture). Second, the hypothesis contains an implicit

Marcionism, named after the "Church heretic" of the second century CE who picked the parts of the Bible he found congenial as the true parts, and programmatically dismissed the rest of the text.

It has to be recognized that both of these strategies have considerable merit. There is no doubt that "human projection" functions in the articulation of God, though we are not usually very ready to admit that even our "best theology" (orthodoxy!) is also an act of human projection. There is no doubt, moreover, that in the biblical text YHWH is always breaking new ground and "doing a new thing." For that reason it is not a surprise that God changes and takes on fresh form. At the very least, I suspect, it might be recognized that such "development" in the character of God was neither an obvious matter nor a unilateral development. Rather every newness concerning God entailed hard resolved work, because the character of God is not readily supple. The hard work is a dialogical interaction between the imaginative initiatives of the interpreters and the push-back from the resilient character of God already known in text and in the community. That resilience, insofar as it is credited as theological datum, precludes easy dismissal as human projection, either of a patriarchal harshness or a counter to such patriarchal harshness. God's character is shaped and reshaped through participation in the open-ended happenings that constitute the story of the world, and is not to be remade according to interpretive whim. Readers may find these two strategies adequate for "explaining away" divine violence; many have found them to be so. I do not find them adequate, even though they are serious strategies to be taken seriously.

III.

I find such "explanations" for divine violence too easy, because we in the church finally respond to the Bible as "revelation," that is, as a disclosure of the long life that God has lived in the history of the world. After we have taken seriously "human projection" and "evolution," we still say concerning the Bible, "The Word of the Lord ... Thanks be to God." We are still left with the God who is witnessed as enacting *violence on behalf of chosen Israel* and *violence in the maintenance of divine honor and assertion of divine rule*. The God who is a real character and an active agent in the narrative of the world has a history of violence that I think cannot be denied or explained away. This is something of who God has been in our past; it does not, in my judgment, serve us well to pretend otherwise.

YHWH

On the assumption that the violence of God is real theological data (and not simply human projection to be easily dismissed and not simply primitivism to be superseded), that leaves us with the hard work of theological processing of that memory of God and the residue of hurt that ensues from that memory. I suggest three responses to redress that history of divine violence. These responses are perhaps not unlike those required of a family that continues to face a residue of hurt from a family member who has hurt, abused, or shamed others in addictive ways. The work is important because wounding caused by the violence of God can perhaps be seen at the core of faith Thus Jews (and Christians along with them)—in the wake of the Shoah—must continue to ponder how God could perpetrate (or at least permit the perpetration of) such violence against God's own people. And for Christians recent study has made us aware that "redemption on the cross" in the execution of Jesus can be understood as an act violence by the Father against the Son, an act that extends the pernicious notion of "redemptive violence." In light of such problematics that must concern both Jews and Christians, the following responses seem both possible and required of us, given our remembered past with God.

1. We may *practice honesty* about that past that includes God's performance of violence, and not engage in denial about it. The truth given in the text is that God is deeply enmeshed in the performance of violence, and we cannot pretend otherwise. This is a God, says the tradition, who has abused, shamed, and wounded in recurring patterns; it is our tradition and we may not deny it!

2. We may *engage in repentance* for the wounding inflicted by God, perhaps to include gestures of reparation. And if we cannot fully accept that the wounding is of God, then it is enough to deal with the wounding inflicted by God's people (including the church) on many people. Thus in my church, the United Church of Christ, the national Church has articulated an apology to the native peoples of Hawaii for the exploitation enacted by our missionaries, no doubt in the name of God if not at the behest of God. Such repentance is at the outset honest acknowledgment, but more active and practical redress is in order.

3. We may *issue petitions and protests* to God, petitions that God should exhibit and perform God's better self toward the world and its vulnerable peoples, protests that God should be reprimanded and summoned to account for abusive actions. Such prayers would be in the train of those voiced by Moses. In Exod 32:11–14, after Aaron's failure with the Golden

Calf and God's huge anger against Israel, Moses "prays God back" from harsh retaliation against Israel. He does so by appealing to God's self-regard. In a second such prayer, amid the food crisis in the wilderness, Moses again vigorously petitions God to choose a better course of action. Moses makes an appeal based on God's own self-declaration in Exod 34:6–7 (Num 14:13–19). God is "almost persuaded" by the prayers of Moses (vv. 20–25). In the wake of Moses' courage, prayers of protest and petitions for divine redress show up in the Psalms and in Jeremiah. They are premised on the conviction that "God" is not a code-word for something else; rather the petitions and protests pertain to the real character and agent who is called to account for actions that God's own people find intolerable.

To the extent that the violence of God is a serious theological datum, God's people are not permitted to be passive, indifferent, or uncritical in the face of such perpetration. We may not be bystanders, but have a role to play in urging God to be truly the God witnessed in the best of the tradition. The human role in summoning God to account is not unlike an "intervention" in which a family "interrupts" an unacceptable performance by a member of the family. Such prayers are indeed *interventions and interruptions* in the practice of God, enacted in the conviction that God can be otherwise than violent. The aim of such work is to evoke a fresh resolve from God to be *God beyond violence* for the sake of the world and, consequently, for the sake of God's own identity and reputation in the world. One can trace in some texts that God resolves to be otherwise. It is that possibility that becomes the ground for hope and trust in God.

Of course if we take the easier path and assume the problem is one of *human projection* or *primitivism*, then we have an easier time of it. But as long as we say "The word of the Lord . . . Thanks be to God" over this book, we may be haunted by more serious reality and more strenuous engagement in the task of interpretation. The tilt of the testimony is that the mercy, fidelity, and compassion of God prevail, but not always and not easily.

3

Class Warfare on Earth and in Heaven

The phrase "class warfare" may be taken as a descriptive term to identify the power dynamics of politics and economics. "Class" refers most often to the gap between the "haves" who enjoy political leverage and economic advantage over the "have-nots" who are vulnerable and relatively powerless. "Warfare" refers to the inescapable tension been "haves" and "have-nots" that most often is covert but occasionally erupts as active hostility in the form of harsh rhetoric or political action. Thus the phrase calls attention to the undeniable realities of social relationships.

But the term is seldom used descriptively. More often it is employed polemically, most often on the lips of "haves." It is then used with reference to any active resistance on the part of "have-nots" that calls attention to inequity. When used in this way, it intends to deny the tension or the gap of power and resources, wanting to suggest social solidarity between "haves" and "have-nots." It is then used to cover over or deny tensions that are inherent in inequitable social relationships. Less often the term is used by "have-nots" to refer to the quiet but effective ways in which "haves" work to keep "have-nots" powerless and resourceless. All of these uses are, in one way or another, part of the tension and problematic of social differentiation on the ground that refuses the cover of noble or polite slogans to the contrary.

Part One. The God to Whom Israel Answers

I.

The phrase, in relation to the Bible, immediately draws the Bible into socio-political, economic reality, so that the Bible can no longer be read "innocently." In order to read the Bible knowingly, it is crucial to understand, as best we can, the socio-economic dynamics that recur in the Bible.

In the Old Testament, that social reality with great consistency consists in a peasant economy of small farmers who lived a tenuous life who faced the concentration of aggressive economic leverage managed by the urban elites in the capital cities of Samaria and Jerusalem. That latter group, presided over by the king, included military leaders, scribes who were the privileged intellectuals of the realm, and priests who presided over the liturgies that legitimated the entire system. Glimpses of this power arrangement are offered in the summaries of the "bureaucracies" of David (2 Sam 8:15–18) and Solomon (1 Kgs 4:1–6), the latter of which concludes with an officer concerned with "forced labor." The report of Solomon's "cabinet" is followed in vv. 7–19 by a list of tax districts, suggesting that the regime was preoccupied with taxation of the peasant economy. The political dynamic consisted in extraction of wealth from the peasants by way of taxation in order to support the indulgent style of the urban elites. Thus in 1 Kgs 12:1–19, the dispute is over taxation. The setup is ripe for tension and "warfare."

In the New Testament the recurring reference to taxation suggests the same dynamic (Matt 17:24; 22:17–19; Luke 2:1–5; Acts 5:37: Rom 13:6–7). In this case the taxes were in the service of Rome. But the power of the Roman Empire depended upon local authorities who were willing to collude, tax collectors as well as priests and scribes who belonged to the local population but who had signed on with the occupying forces. (Thus we may imagine in our own context that Hamad Karzai in Afghanistan is such a local leader who leads at the behest of the occupying empire). Because the "haves" among the urban elites are so powerful, the "have-not" peasants have various strategies of opposition and resistance to such exploitation. In the later Roman context as in the earlier Israelite context, the tension between "haves" and "have-nots" was pervasive and acute. In the Old Testament, moreover, the tension is sometimes presented as one between the Israelites and their Philistine or Canaanite overlords, but the dynamic is the same. Thus for example, in the old poem of Judg 5 where the victory of "the peasants in Israel" is said to be allied with, even synonymous with "the triumphs of the Lord."

> To the sound of musicians at the watering places,
>> there they repeat the triumphs of the LORD,
>> the triumphs of his peasantry in Israel. (Judg 5:11)

YHWH, the God of emancipation, is said to be their ally against the urban power structure that threatened its viability.

II.

To some great extent the Old Testament appears to be the offer of faith on the lips of the "have-not" peasants who dare to articulate class tension in loud voice as though it is a tension that pertains is heaven as well as on earth. That is, this voice seeks to draw YHWH into the social crisis on the assumption that YHWH is not a neutral or even-handed reference point. That is, they recruit YHWH into the class warfare in which they see themselves as victims and not perpetrators of the war.

1. The *laments, complaints, and protests of the Psalter* are most commonly voices from below that seek to summon YHWH into the social struggle. They attempt to recruit YHWH, on the assumption that YHWH is indeed inclined to be in solidarity with such need. The "poor" find themselves at a disadvantage and without resources, and so they appeal as "clients" of YHWH who, if mobilized, will off-set the advantage of the "haves." In Psalm 10, a not uncharacteristic prayer "from below," the attitude, practice, and policy of the "haves" are described for God. This is, of course, a quite partisan and polemical characterization, as the powerful appear to the powerless. They are "the wicked" (vv. 2–3), who are greedy (v. 23), proud (v. 4), "prosperous at all times" (v. 5), and "filled with deceit" (v. 7). On the one hand they are arrogant in their autonomy and do not think they are accountable to God:

> The wicked say, "God will not seek it out";
>> all their thoughts are, "There is no God." . . .
> The think in their heart, "We shall not be moved;
>> throughout all generations we shall not meet adversity."
> They think in their heart, "God has forgotten,
>> he has hidden his face, he will never see it." (Ps 10:4, 6, 11)

The poor imagine what the "haves" think and have on their hearts. On the other hand, not surprisingly, those who scoff at God "persecute the poor" (v. 2), "sit in ambush in the villages" where the peasants live" (v. 8), and "seize the poor" (v. 9). They do so by arrangements concerning mortgages, loans, and taxes. The two points of *mocking God* and *persecuting the poor* go together, because "without God everything is possible." Thus the poetry describes the class war being waged against the vulnerable by those "above."

After that polemical description, the voice of the poor turns to petition and imperative, seeking God's identification with them against the "haves" (v. 12). The "wicked" think they have impunity (v. 13). But the poor know better: "You do see!" (v. 14). Consequently the poor ask God to move violently against the exploitative "haves":

> Break the arm of the wicked and evildoers;
>   seek out their wickedness until you find none. (v. 15)

The prayer ends in confidence that God will act for the most vulnerable:

> O LORD, you will hear the desire of the meek;
>   you will strengthen their heart, you will incline your ear
> to do justice for the orphan and the oppressed,
>   so that those from the earth may strike no more. (vv. 17–18)

There is no way to read such a poem except in the midst of "class warfare." It is for good reason that the church of the "haves" (our church) has silenced such biblical texts, for the poor offer an expose of the way in which power works and the way in which God is known to be a counter power for those without power.

2. For the most part *the prophets of the ninth-seventh centuries* are also voices from below that address the exploitative "haves." Only here, unlike the Psalter, the texts claim not only to be the voice of the poor, but the voice of God who is in solidarity with the vulnerable who are unjustly treated. The "Thus saith the Lord" formula imagines God to be a player in the class conflict.

In the narratives of Elijah and Elisha, there is more action than talk. In 1 Kgs 21, Elisha responds to the royal confiscation of Naboth's land by threatening a violent end to the dynasty (1 Kgs 21:20–24). Elijah, a voice of YHWH, intervenes on the side of the vulnerable peasant farmer to castigate the usurpatious greed of the urban privileged. In doing so, he makes clear that social reality is not simply a contest between the vulnerable "have-nots" and the regent "haves," because YHWH is a third party who will not accept such an arrangement of arrogance. In 2 Kgs 4:1–7, Elisha intervenes on behalf of a resourceless widow. By his intervention he overrides the mortgage system of the economic establishment and rescues the woman from the avarice of the city bankers.

In the more familiar cadences of Amos, Isaiah, Micah, and Jeremiah, the poets know that God will respond to the unregulated avarice of the urban elites. Thus Amos can describe the self-indulgent extravagance of those "at ease in Zion" (Amos 6:4-6). Isaiah can warn about the exploitative economy that seizes the farms of vulnerable peasants in order to amass great estates; Isa 5:8-12). He imagines an agribusiness that so exploits the land that it will not produce. Micah is alert to greedy land practices (Mic 2:1-2). He addresses the urban elites who expect that they can outdistance YHWH in their greed (Mic 3:9). Jeremiah can identify the greedy leaders who have been shameless in their avarice, who recite reassuring mantras of well-being that in fact deny and contradict their devious social reality (Jer 6:13-15).

The prophetic rhetoric is relentless. It insists that YHWH is an upholder of and advocate for justice for the vulnerable. For that reason, no amount of wisdom, wealth, or power can cancel out the neighborly realities of justice and righteousness (Jer 9:23-24). As a third party YHWH, as voiced by the prophets, weighs in decisively on the social map of power. That decisive "weighing in" by prophetic rhetoric alters both the arrogance of the "haves" and the despair of the "have-nots."

3. Given *the cries of the poor* and *the oracles of the prophets, the exodus narrative* functions as the great paradigm for social power in the presence of YHWH. That narrative features Pharaoh as the king-pin of all "haves" who is oppressive and abusive in his insatiable need for accumulation. It also features the "cries" of the peasant-slaves who are completely without social leverage. In their cry, they do not address anyone; they just cry out in their bodily wretchedness (Exod 2:23). But the narrative also features and introduces YHWH as a real character in the plot of history. YHWH is drawn to the cry of the slaves and eventually authorizes and accomplishes the negation of the abusive "haves," thereby creating an alternative future for the "have-nots." The exodus narrative became a styled paradigmatic narrative that can and has been reperformed in many different circumstances. It a script for contemporary enactment of social power. Thus Michael Walzer can say of the Exodus narrative:

— first, that wherever you live, it is probably Egypt;
— second, that there is better place, a world more attractive, a promised land;

> — and third, that "the way to the land is through the wilderness." There is no way to get from here to there except by joining together and marching.[1]

It is this relentless reiteration of the narrative that exhibits YHWH, in the liturgical imagination of Israel, as agent in "class warfare" for the sake of emancipatory justice.

III.

Of course all of these texts—laments, oracles, and narrative—reflect the urgent social agenda of the "have-nots." They are acts of imagination that express hopes and possibilities for the earth. What is daring about biblical faith is that such acts of imagination about earthly possibilities are "kicked upstairs" to become a theological datum. Not only do these lowly peasants hope. YHWH, so these texts declare, hopes and acts with them in solidarity. Nowhere is this more evident than in the ancient poem of Psalm 82. The Psalm imagines a great judicial confrontation in heaven where the many gods are in dispute. The meeting of "the divine council" is presided over by "God," probably the God of Israel who is the creator; the question before the court is the true nature of "godness." The opening speech of the presiding judge makes an accusation against the gods who have not practiced justice, and gives an important mandate for justice for which the gods are responsible:

> Give justice to the weak and the orphan;
>   maintain the right of the lowly and destitute.
> Rescue the weak and the needy;
>   deliver them from the hand of the wicked. (Ps 82:3-4)

The verdict is given that dismisses the failed gods (v. 5). They are sentenced to death because they have failed in their vocation as gods (vv. 6-7). This is an astonishing verdict that insists that emancipatory justice is the measure of divinity.

On the basis of this imagined heavenly court drama, the human spectators address the court in v. 8 and bid the true God, the one who cares about justice, to act. That act of imagination is characteristic in Israel. And of course the witnesses to Jesus assert that he, in the same trajectory, was at work in solidarity with the "have-nots" for the sake of their well-being

---

1. Walzer, *Exodus and Revolution*, 149.

(see Luke 7:22). In this reading, Jesus is present in the class war, a reality anticipated in the song of Mary (Luke 1:52–53). In the short run, Jesus lost the war and was executed by the "haves" with their imperial authority. In the long run, of course, we confess that he prevailed over the lethal "haves" for the sake of the Bethlehem shepherds and their many needy village neighbors.

IV.

This way of reading the text is faithful to my assigned topic. It represents a major trajectory of biblical faith. To be sure, there are many texts in the Bible that do not work in this way, and some that deeply resist this mapping of social reality and divine character around the theme of class warfare. Thus the wisdom tradition of the book of Proverbs (and the witness of Job's friends) are much to the contrary. These texts likely reflect the settled confidence of the "haves" for whom "wisdom" consists in the maintenance of social stability. Already in a very old law, moreover, Israel is warned against "being partial to the poor in a lawsuit" (Exod 23:3).

One can identify a number of texts that witness against "partiality," suggesting an even-handedness that disregards social inequities (Luke 20:21; Acts 10:34; Rom 2:11; Gal 2:6; Eph 6:9; Col 3:2). Such an assertion would to override and silence any of the agitation of class warfare and make a claim that all stand equally before the reality of God. But of course such texts need to be considered in their particularity without using them as a generic dismissal of the facts on the ground that are always germane to every theological claim.

It is clear that the Bible is an arena of contestation between interpretations that in every case reflect social location, social circumstance, and social interest. For the most part, the church of the "haves" has not wanted to notice this contestation about the character of God and the way God is engaged in class warfare.

There is now a well-developed interpretive trajectory concerning God's "preferential option for the poor." That phrasing insists that God is not neutral or even-hand. Rather God has plunged into the middle of social disputes as an advocate. There can hardly be any doubt that the church must reconsider it social location, it social circumstance, its social interest, and its vocation. The astonishing inequity between "haves" and "have-nots" among us is an acute theological datum. There is a reason that the poor people "heard him gladly" (Mark 12:37). Others not so much!

4

Uncoerced Neighborliness amid Predators

EVERYONE SPEAKS OF FREEDOM. No one would think to oppose it. The most passionate liberationists wait for freedom:

> Let freedom ring from Lookout Mountain in Tennessee!
> Let freedom ring from every hill and molehill of Mississippi.
> From every mountainside, let freedom ring. (Martin Luther King, Jr.)

The most zealous national patriot can celebrate our US status as "the leader of the free world." Determined vigilantes can stand at attention while we sing of "the land of the free and the home of the brave," and imagine themselves brave in being free of all governmental imposition. In the end, all-passionate *liberationists, zealous national patriots, and determined vigilantes* can stand side by side and pledge allegiance with a ringing affirmation of "liberty and justice for all." No doubt for some "liberty" is completely defined by "justice," and for others the accent on "liberty" is so great as to slide over the term "justice" without notice.

Clearly in our diverse appeals to freedom, there is some ambiguity or confusion, or simply multiple meanings for the one word. That manifold usage is worth sorting out. It is my judgment that "freedom" has its tap root in biblical faith. But that biblical theme has, in recent centuries in the West, been filtered through the claims of Enlightenment rationality in a way that has decisively modified its meaning. As a result, we are given a spectrum of possible meanings from Bible to Enlightenment, and we each and all take the part of it we prefer, and assume that to be the meaning of the term.

I.

The Enlightenment of the eighteenth century, a major intellectual transformation in Europe, was indeed a moment for freedom, specifically freedom from the imposed collisions of governments and church. The presenting problem was to find a place to stand to in order to interpret the world apart from the "religious wars" that so vexed Europe and that divided, among Catholics and Protestants, theological claims for absolute offers of truth. From that complex development, we may identify three dramatic moments of definition:

1. Rene Descartes, at the turn of the seventeenth century (the same period in which Galileo accomplished his revolutionary work) enacted "a turn to the subject" and away from "objective external authority." His famous declaration, "I think, therefore I am," caused "reality" to pivot on the self's awareness of the self, by implication dismissing all other claims to "objective reality." From Descartes and his mathematical genius stems the "emancipated self" that in our time has issued in endless self-indulgent narcissism.

2. Not so long after the redefining work of Descartes in France, John Locke wrote his remarkable *Essay Concerning Human Understanding*. In his book that deeply informed the thought that led eventually to the US revolution, Locke formulated the "emancipated human person" who had inalienable rights and duties, and whose self is based on experience and reflection on that experience. In the economic sphere Locke judged that the individual person has an unqualified right to his own capacity and his own property with the least possible interference from society, thus "laissez faire" economics. C. B. Macpherson can conclude:

> Locke was indeed at the fountain-head of English liberalism. The greatness of seventeenth-century liberalism was its assertion of the free rational individual as the criterion of the good society; its tragedy was that this very assertion was necessarily a denial of individualism to half the nation.[1]

That "free self" is free,

—from dependence on the will of others;

—from any relations with others except those that serve one's own interests;

---

1. Macpherson, *The Political Theory of Possessive Individualism*, 292.

—for his own person and capacity without owing anything to society.[2]

3. The matter was given more weighty articulation, with different nuance, by Immanuel Kant a century later. Kant's theme of "man come of age" became a charter for emancipation from all traditional thought and all institutional coercion. The sum of this trajectory of thought has been definitive for the modern world, readily embraced by many who have no interest in the philosophical foundations behind much modern freedom.

It requires very little imagination to see in retrospect the political, economic implications of this argument. The traditional alliance of state and church had enacted institutional authority as a safeguard for community coherence and solidarity. With the assertion of emancipated individualism, communal solidarity was greatly weakened, and with it commitment to the "common good." It was now reckoned that the convergence of many individual goods would function, without regulation, for the sake of the common good.

This philosophical trajectory has been variously translated into political theory and into economic practice. Specifically it has been the basis for "free market" thought championed by Milton Freedman and further fictionalized in current popularity by Ayn Rand. In contemporary politics it is perhaps Margaret Thatcher who has given most vivid expression to it in her dictum that "there is no such thing as society; there is only the market." It is this view that has fueled much current political energy and that has legitimated a deregulated consumerism.

What has come along with such unfettered individualism, supported by deregulation, is a predator class of economic players whose prey are the vulnerable, the resourceless, and the marginated. All of that predation is of course done under the flag of "freedom" or even "opportunity," without noticing, as MacPherson does, that it is a "denial of individualism to half the nation." Such disguised predation, in the name of individualism, has permitted and legitimated great concentrations of wealth, social power, and leverage of immense coercive authority on the vulnerable. Modern forms of such "freedom" for the few has led to an authoritarian domination (through financial leveraging, through manipulated law, through ideologically committed media, and through cunning advertising) that is more toxic than the old authoritarianism against which Descartes, Locke, and Kant inveighed.

---

2. Macpherson, *The Political Theory of Possessive Individualism*, 263.

In the name of freedom the modern world has become for many a new situation of despairing bondage.

II.

Behind that modern Enlightenment notion of emancipation stands the biblical witness to covenantal freedom. It is the sad story of the interpretive church, over the centuries, to have entered into an institutional alliance with authoritarian states, and so to package biblical freedom in forms of coercive teaching. It is, then, important in our time of unregulated predation as a form of freedom that we recover and reformulate, as best we can, a biblical notion of covenantal freedom that is served neither by the old authoritarianism of the church nor by modern individualism that is readily confused with gospel freedom.

The biblical account of freedom is rooted in the exodus narrative that Michael Walzer has shown to be the seedbed of all modern revolutions. The context for the narrative is the "unregulated" production system of pharaoh that depended upon "cheap labor" (slavery) (see Exod 5:4–19). That coercive system was disrupted, as the narrative has it, by the God of emancipation who in turn was evoked by the desperate cries of the abused slaves. Thus the cries (Exod 2:23–25) evoked the resolve of God (3:7–9) who in turn recruited and dispatched Moses (3:10) to confront Pharaoh who sat atop the pyramid of coercive power. The cunning narrative of freedom links together *the Holy Resolve of God* and *the human vocation of Moses* that he only reluctantly accepts (3:11—4:17). The narrative knows very well that freedom requires risky human action, here said to be at the behest of the Holy God who wills freedom.

This inescapable conflict over freedom is initiated by the stunning demand of an uncredentialed slave addressed to the defining authority figure, Pharaoh: "Let my people go" (Exod 5:1). This demand is the originary utterance of freedom in the Bible; the demand of Moses is the demand of YHWH, the creator God: God wills freedom! The imperative has an introductory formula, "Thus says YHWH." The initiative is not one from Moses; it is from the lips of YHWH! It is the intent of YHWH before which Pharaoh must ultimately yield, that slave labor should end and that the slaves should be resituated in a viable social circumstance of shalom. The exodus narrative is an account, albeit in liturgical stylized language for the sake of many reperformances in many different circumstances, of the demands of freedom and the failed resistance of Pharaoh to that freedom. The outcome of the narrative, accomplished through tense, contested, dramatic performance, is emancipation and jubilation among the erstwhile slaves (Exod 15:1–18, 20–21).

We are on notice, however, that the imperative, "Let my people go," is only completed with the next phrase, "that they may serve me," elsewhere "that they may worship me," "that they may celebrate a festival to me." The various phrasings are all synonymous. They intend, in sum, that the emancipated slaves should enter into the service of YHWH as an alternative to service to Pharaoh. Thus the freedom enacted in the narrative is an exchange of a *coercive overlord* for a *covenantal overlord*. Or as the later tradition has it: "For they are my *servants*, whom I brought out of the land of Egypt; they shall not be sold as *slaves* are sold" (Lev 25:42). The terms "servants" and "slave" are the same Hebrew word. It is service to YHWH that defines the new freedom to which the narrative witnesses.

We may identify four moments in biblical faith that may be taken as an epitome of the claims of this emancipatory narrative:

1. The second part of the formula, "they may serve me," is enacted and made concrete in the covenant at Mount Sinai (Exod 19–24). The focal point is the Ten Commandments (Exod 20:1–17). Thus emancipation brings Israel into a covenantal relationship that summons to covenantal obedience. The Ten Commandments on the one hand acknowledge YHWH, the Lord of the exodus, as the alternative source of life. This claim marks all other claims to be "the source of life" as pretentious and not credible. The first two commandments protest against the absolutizing of any other claim, theological, political, or economic. On the other hand, the commands aim at protection of the neighbor from abuse and exploitation. Thus the tenth commandment three times uses the word "neighbor," acknowledging that freedom concerns viable neighborliness. In the fourth commandment, moreover, both God and self "rest" in a way that precludes the endless, restless acquisitiveness of Pharaoh. The commandments are in sum an alternative to the commandments of Pharaoh that are all about productive performance.

2. The prophetic tradition of the eighth and seventh centuries voice and advocate a covenantal viability for the community that contradicts the usurpatious practices of the powerful against the weak. They see that something like the oppressive power of Pharaoh is now alive and well in the Israelite political economy. The prophetic indictment is repeatedly against

the king and other leaders who use their leverage to exploit the vulnerable. In Jer 5, for example, such exploitation is a clear and costly violation of that covenantal freedom:

> For scoundrels are found among my people;
>   they take over the goods of others.
> Like fowlers they set a trap;
>   they catch human beings.
> Like a cage full of birds,
>   their houses are full of treachery;
> therefore they have become great and rich,
>   they have grown fat and sleek.
> They know no limits to deeds of wickedness,
>   they do not judge with justice
>   the cause of the orphan, to make it prosper,
>   and they do not defend the rights of the needy.
> (Jer 5:26–28)

The prophets recognize that violation of the covenantal dimensions of freedom will, soon or late, lead to social disaster. The prosperity of the few (in their freedom) at the expense of the many vulnerable, so say the prophets, is an unsustainable illusion.

3. It is a long leap from the prophets to the New Testament witness to Jesus. But Jesus is a child of Judaism and so is fully congruent with the covenantal freedom voiced in the Sinai-prophetic traditions. There is no doubt that Jesus is, in Christian testimony, the great emancipator who liberates folk from all sorts of hindering disabilities. He offers a summary of his emancipatory work: "The blind receive their sight, the lame walk, the lepers are cleansed, the deaf hear, the dead are raised, the poor have good news brought to them" (Luke 7:22). His performance up-ends the old power "givens" in order to make a real life possible for those who have been denied access to such a life. Luke succinctly contrasts the welcome reception of this freedom on the one hand, and the resistance to such freedom embodied among the predator class that intends freedom only for themselves:

> Every day he was teaching in the temple. The chief priests, the scribes, and the leaders of the people kept looking for a way to kill him; but they did not find anything they could do, for all the people were spellbound by what they heard. (Luke 19:47–48)

We may notice, however, that his transformative performance characteristically ended in an imperative: "follow me" (Luke 5:27; 9:59; 18:22).

Uncoerced Neighborliness amid Predators

His offer of an emancipated life did not eventuate in an open-ended individualism. It ended in discipleship! Thus his repeated "follow me" is a belated equivalent to the word among the ancient Hebrew slaves, "that they may serve me." The new freedom given by God is to a new obedience in covenant.

That new obedience, however, is identified by Jesus as "an easy yoke and a light burden" (Matt 11:30). His summons to obedience is a contrast to the exploitative obedience of Pharaoh, of the Roman Empire, or of any exacting religion that colludes with empire. The Bible refuses the notion that freedom is release for autonomy. It is rather a covenantal commitment to care for the neighborly good that makes possible sustainable freedom and well-being for all. Indeed, Jeremiah can assert, on behalf of this tradition, that care for the neighborly good is the form we have of knowing God:

> Did not your father eat and drink
> and do justice and righteousness?
> Then it was well with him.
> He judged the cause of the poor and needy,
> then it was well.
> Is not this to know me?
> says the Lord. (Jer 22:15–16)

4. The apostle Paul is the great voice in the early church for the freedom of the gospel. In the Epistle to the Galatians he invites Jewish Christians and Gentile Christians to be together in the freedom of the gospel:

> So then, friends, we are children, not of the slave but of the free woman. For freedom Christ has set us free. Stand firm, therefore, and do not submit again to the yoke of slavery. (Gal 4:31—5:1)

Brigitte Kahl has recently judged that this mandate to freedom is part of a coded discourse among the enslaved nations about the spirituality and practice of liberation from the Roman "yoke of slavery" (5:1).[3] The epistle, she judges, is an evangelical manifesto against the coercive power of Rome. In our own time, the Gospel is an offer and summons to an alternative to the exploitative system of our society that operates, as did Rome, in the name of freedom.

---

3. Kahl, *Galatians Re-Imagined*, 256.

III.

Thus the issue is joined and remains for us to sort out in faith. Very often "freedom" is a code name for unregulated individualism that permits the strong to override the weak with license for predation. The gospel alternative to that is covenantal engagement wherein true freedom consists in life under the rule of the Lord of the covenant with commands to honor God as ultimate reference point, to deabsolutize the idols, and to protect the neighbor and the neighborhood. It is an "easy yoke," because it is a vision of the common good. The Bible, since its first utterance in the presence of Pharaoh, knows that unrestrained power in the name of freedom is lethal. Covenantal freedom is an alternative offer to all those who are weary and heavy-laden with the performance quotas of Pharaoh who shows up among us in many forms of exploitation.

5

Commanded to Holiness

IT IS A PRIMAL declaration of God in the Bible: "I the LORD your God am holy" (Lev 19:2). The term "holy" pushes us deeply into the mystery of the God of Israel who is without comparison or analogue. The term marks God as "completely other," outside of all of our interpretive or explanatory categories before whom all of our logic fails. The utterance in Lev 19:2 witnesses to God's otherness, separateness, and awesome singularity. Perhaps an effective, even if familiar exposition of God in God's holiness is the hymn:

> Immortal, invisible, God only wise,
> in light inaccessible, hid from our eyes,
> most blessed, most glorious, Ancient of Days,
> almighty, victorious, thy great name we praise.
> Unresting, unhasting, and silent as light,
> nor wanting, nor wasting, thou rulest in might . . .[1]

That hymnic rhetoric, moreover, is matched by a haunting, probing melody that makes the act of praise thick and deep. Without facile current usage of young people, the term "holy" attests to the awareness that God is indeed "awesome," evoking awe.

Israel's experience of God's holiness is given to us in primitive narrative. The God who inhabits the ark proved so dangerous that Israel wanted to expel the ark from its midst. They asked concerning the threat of God:

---

1. Smith, "Immortal, Invisible, God only Wise."

> Who is able to stand before the LORD, this holy God? To whom shall he go so that we may be rid of him? (1 Sam 6:20)

In 2 Sam 6:6–7, moreover, this God struck out in violence against those who touched the ark. The same quality of danger is reflected in the more stately report of Mt. Sinai:

> Be careful not to go up the mountain or to touch the edge of it (Exod 19:12).

Divine holiness permits no easy companionship or intimacy, because this is God for God's self. In Isaiah's vision, the holiness of God is on full exhibit:

> Seraphs were in attendance above him; each had six wings; with two they covered their faces, and with two they covered their feet, and with two they flew. And one called to another and said:
> Holy, holy, holy is the LORD of hosts;
> the whole earth is full of his glory. (Isa 6:2–3)

In response to that awesome vision of God's holiness, Isaiah declares the disqualification of himself and his people: "Woe is me! I am lost, for I am a man of unclean lips and I live among a people of unclean lips" (v. 5). One can see that the rhetoric of Israel, all the way from *primitive narrative* to *stately liturgy*, strives to give expression to the risky "overwhelmingness" of God's person and presence.

The *declarative* statement concerning God in Lev 19:2 is linked to an *imperative* that concerns Israel's conduct and status before this holy God: "You shall be holy." The imperative concerning Israel matches the declaration concerning YHWH. It anticipates that Israel's life shall be congruent with the life of YHWH. The result may be a covenantal connection between the two and a regularized communion that works effectively, even in the face of great risk. The awesomeness of YHWH in holiness marks that presence and that connection as dangerous to Israel. As a result the corresponding holiness of Israel has urgency and must be gotten right!

The Ten Commandments of Exod 20:1–17 provide normative guidelines for the conduct, order, and policies of Israel's life in the world. But the Decalogue itself lacks particularity and so requires interpretation. The sometimes tedious and sometimes vexing repetitions and punctiliousness of the books of Exodus and Leviticus constitute a long-term attempt in Israel to interpret the commands of Sinai in the direction of holiness. They seek to sort out and articulate the conduct and policies of Israel that will qualify Israel to live safely and gladly in the presence of this holy God.

In the book of Exodus, the Sinai covenant is enacted in chapters 19–24. That covenant is broken and renewed in the narratives of Exod 32–34. But between these two narratives are chapters 25–31 (with an enactment as a reprise in chapters 35–40); we have there the instructions given to Moses concerning the construction of the tabernacle as a suitable habitat for YHWH. This text that interrupts the narrative of covenant is filled with endless detail about construction and decoration, about measurements, colors, materials, and workmanship that were to go into the tabernacle. Clearly for the makers and users of this text, enormous attention to detail is the order of the day.

That mass of detail, however, needs to be understood in terms of the intent of the whole, namely, the creation of a space that will be an acceptable, appropriate residence for the holy God, thus a holy place for the holy God presided over by holy priests for the sake of the holy people. The assumption of the text is that this holy God cannot and will not dwell just anywhere, certainly not in a "profane" environment that is judged to be an "abomination," an affront to and a violation of God's character. While such attentiveness may strike one as overdone, one can nevertheless see in our own practice that the maintenance of a "holy place" for the presence of God claims our attention in terms of beauty, order, and loveliness expressed, for example, in flowers and music. The culmination this presentation is the stunning report in Exod 40:34–38 that God does willingly "settle" in the tabernacle that is offered as an alternative to the disordered world where God cannot dwell.

The more difficult texts of the book of Leviticus seek to extend the imperative of holiness that governs the building of the tabernacle, not only to liturgical practice, but also in terms of food, health, sexuality, agriculture, and every domain of community life. The notion of holiness, moreover, is transposed into "cleanness" and "purity" (evident as well in the text of Isa 6). The maintenance of a certain "order" is judge to be appropriate to the presence of God. And what violates that "order" is judged to be a violation of holiness that God's people are to practice.

The temptation in the transposition of *divine holiness* into communal claims of "cleanness" and purity is that every impulse of "disgust" felt by members of the community who make the text are "kicked upstairs" to imagine that what "disgusts" us also "disgusts" God. Such-disgust-become-religious-discipline becomes a method of social control. My friend Richard

Beck has provided a study of the function of "disgust" in religious life.[2] He concludes that there are more-or-less common disgusts about bodily orifices and bodily fluids, so that the management and containment of such bodily matters is generic. But he also notices that disgust is to some large extent socially constructed, and therefore varies from culture to culture. In a reading of the book of Leviticus, we surely have "a recital of disgust" that is in part generic and in part socially constructed that came to functions as an exclusionary principle. It is evident that such a notion of cleanness and purity, based in disgust, may exclude "the other" who is unlike us, with the theological assumption that whom our disgust excludes are, perforce, excluded by the holy God who shares our particular disgust. Thus the rules of disgust may variously concern lepers, menstruating women, those who engage in sexual deviance, but also animals that are cross-bred, fields that have mixed seed, or garments that are synthetic (19:19). The impulse to clarify endlessly the limits of human holiness that is congruent with God produces great and careful detail, all in the service of a passionate theological conviction that functions to curb a world of danger:

> But I have said to you: You shall inherit their land, and I will give it to you to possess, a land flowing with milk and honey. I am the Lord your God; I have separated you from the peoples. You shall therefore make a distinction between the clean animal and the unclean, between the unclean bird and the clean; you shall not bring abomination on yourselves by animal or by bird or anything with which the ground teems, which I have set apart for you to hold unclean. You shall be holy to me; for I the Lord am holy, and I have separated you from the other peoples to be mine. (Lev 20:24–26)

> They shall be holy to you, for I the Lord, I who sanctify you, am holy. (Lev 21:8)

It became the work of the priests (who function as physicians as well) to be the enforcers of distinctions that make possible healthy community and communion with YHWH. In Ezekiel, the priests are judged to be inadequate in making such distinctions that are known to be congruent with the character of God:

> Its priests have done violence to my teaching and have profaned my holy things: they have made no distinction between the holy and the common, neither have they taught the difference between

---

2. Beck, *Unclean*.

> the unclean and clean, and they have disregarded my Sabbaths, so
> that I am profaned among them. (Ezek 22:26)

Such distinctions that eliminate felt disgust becomes a theological principle that has always been seen, by some in the community, to be deeply problematic. Even in the book of Leviticus, the remarkable chapter 19 goes in a quite different direction and suggests that neighborliness, not uncleanness, is the ground and measure for covenantal connection to YHWH.

In important ways the early church in the New Testament struggled with the holiness traditions of Israel that had become an exclusionary principle. Specifically the question in the church came to concern the inclusion of Gentiles who were in principle excluded from the holy people Israel, an issue already concretely but inchoately pressed upon Jesus in Mark 7:26–29 concerning a "Gentile" woman. The issue is joined directly in Acts 10:9–16 wherein Peter, in a trance, was commanded to "kill and eat" all kinds of "four-footed creatures and reptiles and birds of the air. Peter had dreamed that he was being pushed by the power of God outside the comfort zone of his "disgust" that had been articulated in the holiness traditions of Leviticus. It must have been "disgusting" to eat such forbidden foods. But the trance culminates in a divine dictum: "What God has made clean you must not call unclean" (Acts 10:15). This dictum amounts to an overthrow of the holiness regulation. The trance concerns unclean food. The narrative context, however, indicate that Peter's nightmare was about welcoming the Gentiles into the community of the church, the Gentiles who were unclean and who evoked disgust. The narrative concerns the long-standing, liturgically legitimated definition of cleanness that sustained a distinction between outsiders and insiders, between the accepted holy ones and the unacceptable others:

> You yourselves know that it is unlawful for Jews to associate with
> or to visit a Gentile; but God has shown me that I should not call
> anyone profane or unclean. (v. 28)

The remarkable turn of the narrative is articulated on the lips of Peter. The very one who has defen ded the purity distinction now becomes a lead witness in opening the circle of faith out beyond the "pure." It is from this narrative turn that the church is opened to Gentiles, the very ones who did not practice holiness. The force of this transformation is voiced by Paul in his complex (tortured?) argument in Rom 9–11 concerning Jews and Gentiles together in the church, about which he declares:

Part One. The God to Whom Israel Answers

> The scripture says, No one who believes in him will be put to shame; for there is no distinction between Jew and Greek; the same Lord is Lord of all and is generous to all who call upon him. For, "Everyone who calls on the name of the Lord shall be saved." (Rom 10:11–13)

The old principle of disgust, cast as cleanness and purity, is overcome for the sake of a new inclusiveness.

Given that radical turn of affairs, we may ask then if the church, in its sense of the Gospel, gave up on the notion of practicing holiness that seeks congruity with the holiness of God. And of course, the answer is "no"; the church did not abandon its vocation of holiness; in subsequent symbols we have come to confess the church as "one, holy, apostolic, catholic." "Holiness" is always a mark of the faithful church.

What that mark of holiness signifies is of course endlessly contested in the church. We may ask, did the trance of Peter and the dictum of Paul eliminate the role of "being holy" in ways that are commensurate with the holiness of God? One can see, in the later epistles of the New Testament, that the church has continued to be preoccupied with its own holiness, though now the matter is radically recharacterized. The following texts will indicate new directions in the church it has pondered the old commands of holiness. In what is likely a baptismal formula, the letter to the Ephesians states:

> You were taught to put away your former life, your old self, corrupt an deluded by its lusts, and to be renewed in the spirit of your minds, and to clothe yourselves with the new self, created according to the likeness of God in true righteousness and *holiness* (Eph 4:22–24)

The new self is constituted by "righteousness and *holiness*. That in turn is exposited in this way:

> Put away from you all bitterness and wrath an anger and wrangling and slander, together with all malice, and be kind to one another, tenderhearted, forgiving one another as God in Christ has forgiven you. (Eph 5:31)

> As God's chosen ones, *holy* and beloved, clothe yourselves with compassion, kindness, humility, meekness, and patience. Bear with one another and, if anyone has a complaint against another, forgive each other; you also must forgive. Above all, clothe

> yourselves with love, which binds everything together in perfect harmony. (Col 3:12–15)
>
> Like obedient children, do not be conformed to the desires that you formerly had in ignorance. Instead, as he who called you to be holy, *be holy* yourselves in all your conduct; for as it is written, "You shall be holy, for I am holy. (1 Pet 1:14–16)

The epistles go far in recharacterizing holiness as the capacity to maintain a generous community amid genuine conflict. In a deeply disputatious society, that may be a primal witness to the holiness of God in God's holy church.

It is likely that the church will continue to dispute issues of holiness, most especially concerning matters of sexuality. The ground for such dispute is provided in the fact that at the same time in the early church a) attended to issues of holiness but b) moved beyond old content in its fresh articulation of holiness. It would be easy enough, as has often been done in the church, to reduce holiness to a catalogue of requirements that simply reflect our particular "disgusts" that are then assigned to God. It is much more of a challenge to recognize that the old exclusions of the "other" have been overcome in the Gospel. The church has a long history of practicing exclusion in the name of holiness. We in the dominant church have long regarded African Americans as "unclean." Now we are in a moment of dispute about the "cleanness" of gays and lesbians; disgust still runs high against that particular "other."

We are, as always, left with the hard work of sorting out the practice of holiness. What we have always to keep in purview is our temptation to elevate our disgust to divine preference, so that the embrace of the other is the nonnegotiable on-going summons of the Gospel. The practice of holiness as being in sync with the holy God may indeed consist in the embrace of the other whom God has embraced beyond our conventional disgust. The church, as always, is engaged in unlearning our parochial fears in the staggering awareness that God is no practitioner of our particular parochial fears. The work of holiness is to continue to struggle with such hard distinctions and to see at the same time that holiness invites to forgiveness and reconciliation. These old epistles bid the church always to remember its mandate and its grounding in the God of forgiveness.

II

The Human Self as Member and Failure

6

The Human Self

A Member, not a Private Operator

IN A CULTURE OF "selfies" it is important to reflect on the nature of the self who is an endless enigma to us. The self was already an enigma to the earliest singers of the book of Psalms who asked in amazement, "What is man?" (in familiar traditional translation),"What is humankind? What is the human person?" The Psalm recognizes the odd location of the human self, given dominion over all of creation, and entrusted with immense authority; at the same time, however, that same self is accountable to God who has overriding dominion, who evokes glad self-yielding praise to God as the self is relativized to the power of God. The recognition at the same time of *having dominion* and *being answerable* means that the human person is inescapably caught up in a relationship with God from whom life comes and to whom life is lived back in celebrative exuberance.

I.

When we press further in the book of Psalms, we find in Psalm 139 a quite remarkable exposition of the human self before God. The psalm begins, even though it is about the human self, with a series of "you" statements concerning God that begins with an abrupt address, "LORD" (YHWH):

II. The Human Self as Member and Failure

You have searched,
> You search,
>> You know,
>>> You discern,
>>>> You know,
>>>>> You hem in,
>>>>>> You lay (vv. 1–5)

It is all about God's initiative! This is followed by series of questions and statements dominated by the first person pronoun, "I":

Where can I go?
> Where can I flee?
>> If I ascend,
>>> If I make,
>>>> If I take,
>>>>> If I say. (vv. 7–11)

But even these sentences ostensibly dominated by "I" culminate with "your spirit, your presence, you, you, your hand, your right hand, you (vv. 7–11). Everywhere the "I" statements end with "you. Everything about the self ends with reference to God.

The dramatic movement of this Psalm is completed with a return to "you" sentences:

You formed,
> You knit,
>> Your works,
>>> Your eyes
>>>> Your book,
>>>>> Your thoughts
>>>>>> You (vv. 13–17)

And the final phrase of this reflection is:

> I come to the end—I am still with you. (v. 18)

The Human Self

This Psalm remarkably traces the movement from "you" (God) (vv. 1–5) to "I" (the human self) (vv. 7–12) and back to "you" (God) (vv. 13–18). The human self is enveloped in the mysterious, inscrutable generative force of God. Thus in a much more elemental reflection the affirmation of Psalm 139, apparently wrought out of anguish rather than out of exuberance, echoes the doxology of Psalm 8. Human life is inextricably linked to the life and rule of God, and that connection is inescapable. In Psalm 8 that connection is a wonder because of which the psalmist is dazzled and grateful. In Job 7:17–21, a parody of Ps 8, that same inescapability is a wearisome burden, because Job want to be left alone and left unmonitored by God. But as either dazzlement and gratitude or as vexing burden, the God-connection is non-negotiable for the human self.

II.

We may set it down that in biblical affirmation human life is *a gift from God*, wholly dependent on God, fully constituted by gifts that the human self cannot generate for the self. In an originary and elemental formulation, it is asserted in the second creation narrative that the human person is constituted from "the dust of the earth" (Gen 2:7). The human self is elementally and fundamentally material in origin. That "dust," moreover, of itself possesses no life force. It may come to life only as the creator God breathes on the dust, thereby enlivening the dust. That act of generative divine breath eventuates in a "living being," a full human self. The singers of the psalms knew that that initiating and sustaining breath is a gift and can never be a human possession or a human achievement. It is a faithfully given gift of God that is totally in God's governance. The human self receives the human self from God:

> When you hide your face, they are dismayed;
>   when you take away their *breath*, they die
>   and return to their dust.
> When you send forth your *spirit*, they are created;
>   and you renew the face of the ground. (Ps 104:29–30)

These verses are even more poignant when it is recognized that the same term rendered "breath" and "spirit" in the two verses is the same Hebrew term, "breath, wind, spirit" (*ruah*).

II. The Human Self as Member and Failure

The singers of the psalms regularly returned to and did not forget the origin of the human self in this elemental narrative of Gen 2. And the church regularly returns to this Genesis tale of origin in the Good Friday mantra, "Remember, you a dust." Thus the psalmist can say,

> As a father has compassion for his children,
>   so the Lord has compassion for those who fear him.
> For he knows how we were made;
>   he remembers that we are dust. (Ps 103:13–14)

The older translation has it, "He remembers our frame," that is, how we were "formed" from the dust. God remembers the narrative of Gen 2:7! God remembers that we were made from dust and require God's faithfully given breath in order to live. God remembers the frailty and vulnerability of the human self; that memory on God's part evokes compassion by the father of a motherly kind. In that same Psalm, the singers gladly recite how faithful God is in sustaining life through steadfast love." The term is used in this Psalm four times (vv. 4, 8, 11, 17). The faithfulness of God guarantees the instant-by-instant generative force of breath that enlivens our feeble dust. That divine reliability is the secret of human life.

III.

As human is a gift from God, so human life is to be *lived back to God* in gladness. On the one hand, life is lived back to God in exuberant self-giving praise. Praise is a glad recognition human life is penultimate and is always referred back to the giver of life who is ultimate. Thus the singers of the psalms end the collection of the Psalter with a torrent of praise as acknowledgement of the goodness and generosity of God (Pss 145–150). The singer address the God

> who builds Jerusalem.
>   who gathers the outcasts,
>   who heals,
>   who binds up,
>   who determines,
>   who lifts up,
>   who casts down (Ps 147:2–6);

> who covers,
>> who prepares,
>>> who gives,
>>>> who takes (vv. 8–11)
> who strengthens,
>> who blesses,
>>> who grants,
>>>> who fills,
>>>>> who sends,
>>>>>> who gives,
>>>>>>> who scatters,
>>>>>>>> who hurls,
>>>>>>>>> who sends out,
>>>>>>>>>> who makes,
>>>>>>>>>>> who declares (vv. 12–19)

In highly stylized form the verbs concern the wonder of the creator and creation and the fidelity of God to Israel. All of this is gladly acknowledged. The doxologies of Israel function to refuse the notion that the self is autonomous and self-made or self-sufficient.

On the other hand, life is handed back to God through glad obedience. Thus the Psalms are introduced by a summons to "meditate on the Torah day and night," a meditation that is the clue to "prospering" (Ps 1:2–3). This obligation to obey Torah is a refusal of the notion that the self can do whatever it wants and have its own way. The human self in the Psalter does not imagine that obedience will produce blessing and life as though it were a *quid pro quo* transaction. Rather obedience is a glad and willing response to gift of life already generously given by God, an obedience that is the completion of the transaction of life in glad acknowledgement. Without that obedience, the gift is left unacknowledged and the transaction is left unresolved and incomplete.

Living life in obedience as an act of handing life gladly back to God is not a flat adherence to rules and requirements. It is rather an elongated, strenuous process of interpretation, negotiation, a back-and-forth process

II. The Human Self as Member and Failure

about the responsible ways in which the gift can be honored and enhanced. This means, in the context of Israel's Torah and Christ's commands, that the *rules* are in the service of the *relationship*, and the relationship is a zone of dynamic freedom so that the obedient person must take on responsibility for on-going interpretation in order to match and engage with the generous sovereignty of God. Thus the human self, in receiving life as a faithfully given gift is marked by a full enactment of *praise* (that refuses self-sufficiency) and *obedience* (that refuses autonomy).

IV.

But of course the self who sings the psalms is not an isolated individual. The psalms-self is a participant in "the great congregation" into which the self is born and in which the self gladly participates (Pss 22:22, 25; 35:18; 107:32; 149:1). That participation, moreover, is a long process of being summoned, shaped, and nurtured to a full mature self. The birthed self has no chance of becoming a full human self without a receiving caring community of nurture. This social dimension of the human self is a refusal of every notion a lone self before God or a lone self in the world. In the horizon of the Psalter, we are never alone before God but we are always in the company of the neighbors who constitute the Great Congregation. The sociology of the ancient world (and indeed the on-the-ground sociology of the contemporary world, despite ideological notions to the contrary) makes clear that a full self is a social self, evoked and formed by the community.

—The social self is born into *a narrative* of creation and deliverance that the congregation recites; the new human self inhales that narrative even before any conscious recognition. It is for that reason that one can observe very young children in church gladly mouthing the confessions and prayers of the church, receiving a self by osmosis from the community. Human life consists in participation in and contribution to the open-ended narrative of the community in which God, the giver of life, is known to be a full participant. It is for that reason that Israel is commanded by Moses, "Tell your children in time to come . . ." (Exod 12:26–27; 13:8). What they are to be told is the fundamental narrative of rescue whereby YHWH has constituted a particular, concrete, self-aware company that is grounded in gift and pledged in obedience.

—That narrative is the compelling, normative *memory* of the community, so that the human self is a remember. Such remembering is an urgent contrast to the reductionist modernist practice of amnesia among us signified by the delete button. That narrative memory does not depend on the assent of the new self, because it was a stylized telling before the new self can give assent. The memory includes the great normative wonders of God, but it also includes quirky details of inexplicable heroes and sages and shameful details of past violence, all of which are present in the self-forming community.

—That normative narrative includes buoyant *hope* because the storytelling community trusts that God has made promises and is faithful to keep those promises. Thus the Psalmic-self constitutes a refusal of despair because the self is formed to trust and know that there are more good gifts to be given by the giver of all good gifts:

> This is my comfort in distress,
> > that your promise gives me life
> (Ps 119:50; see vv. 49, 74, 81, 114)

The narrative is the story of traveling with neighbors, brothers and sisters, to whom obligations are owed. The narrative is designed, by the power of memory and hope, to invite the new self to *habits and disciplines* that honor the creator God and that enhance the community and the world in which the new self is located. In the book of Psalms those habits and disciplines are constituted by the Torah upon which the new self is summoned "to meditate day and night" (Ps 1:2).

Thus on all counts the human self is evoked, constituted, and cherished by an adult community that intends a new self

Who *shares a normative narrative* that tells against *autonomy*;

Who shares in *a normative memory* that tells against *amnesia*;

Who shares in *a normative hope* that tells against *despair*, and

Who shares in *normative habits* that tell against *narcissistic self-indulgence*.

This self, it will be readily seen, is a counter-self, counter to the easy assumptions and uncritical practices of a society like ours that imagines an autonomous self who exists only for one's self. This socially constructed self is a creature of and for relational engagement for which the biblical word is "covenant." The covenantal self is both sustained and summoned by God the giver of life; that social self is always summoned and sustained by and for the community into which the new self is born on its way to fullness.

V.

It will be seen that I have said nothing about the biological origins of the self or the biological endings of the self. And therefore I have said nothing about the current dispute about abortion, about the "right to life" or "freedom of choice," or the current question about "end of life" issues. The community of the Psalms was not preoccupied with such issues and did not use its energy biological questions. Nor did it have the biological data or understandings that we have are grounded in modern science. For that reason I do not think that the Psalms, or the Bible for that matter, can be mobilized in *any direct way* about these issues; and when it is mobilized in *an indirect way*, the tradition of the text is filtered through a thicket of interpretive judgments. But surely the text of the Psalms invites us to think thickly about these matters and not rest on easy notions of the self. I suggest that the characterization of the self I have traced on the basis of the Psalms is an important alert to any thinking for either the right to life or freedom of choice.

The "right to life" movement tends to think and speak of the new life (at whatever point it originates) as that new life in and of itself had an absolute "right to exist" without reference to any contextual reality. But that advocacy most often does not consider the communal formation of the self, but ends its advocacy at birth without any awareness that a fully formed self requires a community, a social practice, and a social policy concerned for a self coming only slowly and by hard attentive work to a fully matured self. That the argument in its most popular forms imagines an autonomous self with autonomous worth without reference to communal work that is indispensable for the full arrival a mature self.

Conversely the "freedom of choice" movement for the most part talks only about the individual exercise of unencumbered, unhindered personal freedom for the potential mother without communal context. As the right to life movement imagines *the new self* as an autonomous agent, so the freedom of choice movement talks as if *the pregnant woman* were an autonomous self. Insofar as such autonomy marks the argument, it is a betrayal from both sides concerning the social self that requires thick engagement in a community that concerns both the life given by God and the life lived back to God. Both the new life and the life of the woman are set in the midst of social reality that cannot be set aside for the sake of an easier contention.

In the same way "end of life" issues cannot be reduced simply to biological questions unless they are situated in the fabric of the community. In the Old Testament and in the Psalms "life" is characterized by fullness of capacity and strength and death is an absence of such capacity and strength. In the rhetoric of Israel, moreover, any diminishment of full life, (such as hunger, poverty, or social isolation) is said to be "death," and any enhancement (such as food, resource, social inclusion) is said to be restoration of "life." Thus "life and death" are not absolute states, but are on a spectrum from fullness to emptiness, from strength to weakness, from vitality to exhaustion. When we treat "life and death" as absolute states, we to tend to reduce end of life issues to biological viability. Against such reductionism, when the quality of one's life is diminished, one may say it is a dying. A recognition of that dynamic characterization of life and death frames end of life issues very differently and defies the temptation to reduce human life to a sustainable commodity.

VI.

The assumptions of the modern self marked by *amnesia, autonomy, despair, and radical individualism* constitute a durable and destructive force in our society. That intense temptation to "possessive individualism" evidenced in consumerism is, in general, anti-neighborly in practice and in policy. Thus in our commodity-propelled society, there is a deep and intense antagonism for many who are candidates for "neighbor" . . . immigrants, the poor, Muslims and gays. All such persons are potential neighbors who are negatively discounted because the social embedment of the self in a social fabric is not taken seriously.

Psalm 73 is a script for a self who had well nigh been seduced into the commodity rat race with its "virtues" of celebrity, cynicism, wealth, and despair. The psalmist acknowledges that "my foot had almost slipped" into envy of those who were successful in the commodity rat-race (v. 2). Only at the last moment (!) the psalmist, in a stunning turn of critical awareness (v. 18) came to recognize that those who succeeded in the commodity rat-race had no sustainable future:

> Truly you set them I slippery placer;
> > you make them fall to ruin.
> How they are destroyed in a moment,
> > swept away utterly by terrors!
> They are like a dream when one awakes;
> > on awakening you despise their phantom. (Ps 73:18–20)

The psalmist having been restored to sanity, having "come to himself" (see Luke 15:17), recognizes that his true life is otherwise. His is a life in the company of the God who is "my portion forever" (Ps 73:26). The psalmist returns to his community of hope (v. 24) and to the great congregation of praise (v. 28).

The church has an immense stake in this distinctive sense of self that is a refusal of the values of a "selfie culture." That distinctive sense of self as a social construction in response to the wonder of God requires more than political slogans or pious mantras. That self requires a *community of attentiveness* and the generation of a *social infrastructure* of sustenance that cares for and serves not only the powerful and successful, but also the vulnerable who are readily left behind when the covenantal reality of human existence is scuttled by the mantras of market commoditization. We are not labeled and branded. We are named and treasured in our rituals of immersion.

7

Obedience

Why Obey, Whom to Obey, How to Obey

IN BIBLICAL HORIZON, THE covenanted self is socialized into a particular set of habits and disciplines, and under obligation to perform those habits and disciplines. Serious relationships inescapably bring with them expectations that amount to obligation. When the relationship functions well, the performance of such obligations in specific habits and disciplines is more *delight* than *duty*. The fact that relationships entail obligations is evident in our most intimate relationships such as marriage or the relation of parent and child. In a marriage, regardless of how much romantic love is present at the outset, it very soon emerges that the partner imposes expectations that have more or less imperative force. In a parent child relationship, the parent discovers from the outset that the treasured child imposes obligations that are of an immediately bodily sort that cry out (literally) for obedient performance. Before very long, moreover, the child learns that the love of the parent imposes expectations. These expectations may be received and enacted in a willing generous way, or as D. W. Winnicott has seen, in a false and manipulative way. In either mode, they are urgent.

I.

The matter of a relationship eventuating in obligatory expectations is much more specific in the tradition of ancient Israel. In its core narrative, the exodus emancipation is wonder that evokes the dancing joy of Israel (Exod 15:20–21). It is not very long, however, before the emancipatory God who has taken Israel as "my firstborn son" (Exod 4:22) enunciates clear expectations that have the force of command. Thus in Exod 19, a narrative report separated by only the three chapters of the wilderness sojourn from the exodus drama (Exod 16–18), the emancipatory God asserts the conditional "if" upon which the future of Israel is premised:

> Now therefore, if you obey my voice and keep my covenant, you shall be my treasured possession out of all the peoples. (Exod 19:5)

The tacit negative counterpoint to this statement is that if Israel does not "listen" (obey), it will not be YHWH's treasured possession. Israel, grateful for deliverance from the unbearable coercion of Pharaoh, eagerly assents to the commands of YHWH, even before they are articulated (Exod 19:8). It is only after that ready assent that the commandments articulate the obligatory expectation YHWH has of the covenantal community, and thus of the covenanted selves as members of the community who are thereby inducted into the emancipated community of obligation (Exod 20:1–17). That set of nonnegotiable expectations begins in Exod 20:1 by connecting the commandments to the memory of emancipation:

> I am the LORD your God, who brought you out of the land of Egypt, out of the house of bondage. (Exod 20:1)

It is the exodus memory that propels the commandments, that identifies the God who speaks the commandments and inducts this community into ready obedience. That readiness is indicated in the oath of allegiance in Exod 24:4, 7:

> All the words that the LORD has spoken we will do . . . All that the Lord has spoken we will do and we will be obedient.

The emancipated selves as members of the emancipated community are under obligation, willing obligation, in order to sustain an ongoing emancipatory vision and practice that echoes and reiterates the initial liberation from Egyptian slavery. The commandments persist over time and through the generations because they are the covenantal, nonnegotiable expectations of the Lord of the exodus. Thus the covenanted self, socialized into the drama of Sinai, is inducted into commandments that are, when properly engaged, healthy, because they reflect and perform the imperatives of emancipation.

II.

That dramatic, ongoing process of socialization into the commandments of Sinai as the expectation of the emancipatory God characteristically takes place in a cultural context where the dominant social expectations (habits and disciplines) are quite to the contrary. The force of dominant social expectations and obligations is immense, and seeks to socialize all persons into its orbit, so that the peculiar obligations of the covenanted selves in covenanted community are characteristically in deep tension with dominant habits and disciplines.

In my essay ("The Human Self") I have articulated some of these dominant habits, disciplines, and obligations. Among them I have included amnesia, denial, autonomy, despair, and isolated individualism. For the most part these habits are unrecognized and uncritically embraced among us, even though they are, in systemic ways, unhealthy.

To be sure, the habits and disciplines of amnesia, denial, autonomy, despair, and isolated individualism do not closely correspond to the apparatus of violence of Pharaoh from which the slaves were emancipated. *Mutatis mutandis*, however, the greedy anxious pursuit by Pharaoh of commodities (grain, storehouse cities, bricks), all made possible by cheap labor comes close enough to our present circumstance that we can readily, with some imagination, transfer Israel's core narrative of bondage and emancipation to our own context. The predatory economy of our context, with its illusionary assurances, is an echo and reiteration of the system of Pharaoh. Pharaoh's system of the predatory economy required the reduction of neighbor to helpless cheap labor (Gen 47:13–25). The Exodus–Sinai drama, propelled by YHWH, was alternative to Pharaoh, and contradicted and interrupted Pharaoh's systemic claims. It is no wonder that this narrative of emancipation came to require alternative habits and disciplines in order to resist the abusive hegemony of Pharaoh.

III.

The memory of Sinai is the beginning of a process of articulating and embracing alternative habits and disciplines in the form of commandments. Israel came to know quickly that relationship with YHWH brought with it obligatory expectations upon which the relationship depended:

II. The Human Self as Member and Failure

> The Israelites' opportunity to demonstrate their love for the Lord are vastly more numerous, effectively encompassing the whole of heir communal life. Good deeds become acts of personal fidelity, faithfulness to the personal God, and not simply the right things to do within some supposedly universal code of ethics (though they may be that as well.). Conversely, bad deeds become acts of betrayal, akin . . . to adultery. They are not simply morally wrong in the abstract; they wrong the divine covenant partner.[1]

At Sinai the Ten Commandments are a declaration by YHWH of obligations that will make it possible to sustain a viable political economy outside the control and purview of Pharaoh. The covenanted self is nurtured in these alternative commandments so that the self has the capacity to live outside the predatory requirements of Pharaoh. We can observe that socialization process in the Mosaic instruction of Deut 6:20–24:

> When your children ask you in time to come, "What is the meaning of the decrees and the statutes and the ordinances that the Lord your God has commanded you?" then you shall say to your children, "We were Pharaoh's slaves in Egypt, but the Lord brought us out of Egypt with a mighty hand. The Lord displayed before our eyes great and awesome signs and wonders against Egypt, against Pharaoh and all his household. He brought us out from there in order to bring us in, to give us the land he promised on oath to our ancestors. Then the Lord commanded us to observe all these statutes, to fear the Lord our God, for our lasting good, so as to keep us alive, as is now the case.

The children are confronted with "decrees, statutes, and ordinances." When they asked, they learned that these obligations are given by the Lord of the exodus who is keeping ancestral promises. Thus the ground of the commandments is in memory. The future expectation, however, is for "our lasting good, so as to keep us alive." The habits and disciplines of Torah make life possible. Without them, so says the tradition, comes death and loss of land. Of course the commodity ideology of Pharaoh, reperformed in what is called "Canaanite" modes, promises to the contrary that life is guaranteed by consent to and participation in the predatory economy with its insatiable requirements of production and performance. Israel is always faced with these alternatives; the self socialized into Torah habits has

---

1. Levenson, *The Love of God*, 14.

ground and capacity for resistance to that predatory ideology that wants to nullify the exodus and eliminate the chance for neighborliness.

It is conventional to find in the Ten Commandments two "tablets" of obligation (Exod 20:1–7). On the one hand the first three commandments pertain to the holiness of the exodus God who is not to be compromised by divided loyalty (v. 3), who is not to be reduced to manageable commodity (vv. 4–6), and who is not to be mobilized in the service of "vain" projects (v. 7). The import of these commandments is to place YHWH the emancipator beyond all domestication, and to recognize the ultimacy of YHWH that makes all other loves and loyalties penultimate and of lesser moment. Thus YHWH is incomparable, unlike any other. The great disobedience for this set of commandments is idolatry, the attempt to domesticate YHWH, to reduce YHWH to manageable scope, and so to draw too close to the inscrutable mystery of the emancipatory God.

The second "tablet" of the Ten Commandments concerns human relationships, and draws a vigorous line against intrusion into the security, dignity, or respect of other members of society (Exod 20:8–17). The tenth commandment, the prohibition against acquisitiveness, has in purview the neighbor, that is, a fellow member of the community (v. 17). The term "neighbor" is used three times in this terse commandment; the prohibition recognizes that the "other" in society, by his/her very presence, imposes limitation on the actions of the self. The prohibitions against killing, adultery, stealing and false court testimony indicate that the "other" in society is a non-transgressable restraint upon the self who may seek otherwise seek to maximize the force of the self at the expense of the neighbor (vv. 13–16).

Thus the two tablets" situate the covenanted self in two defining relationships, toward God and toward neighbor. Or in the rhetoric of Jesus, these are "the two great commandments," one a quote from Lev 19:18 on love of neighbor and the other a quote from Deut 6: on love of God:

> Then the scribe said to him, "You are right, Teacher; you have truly said that 'he is one, and besides him there is no other'; and 'to love him with all the heart and with all the understanding, and with all the strength,' and 'love one's neighbor as oneself'—this is much more important than all whole burnt offerings and sacrifices. When Jesus saw that he answered wisely, he said to him, 'You are not far from the kingdom of God." (Mark 12:32–33)

This is such familiar territory to us that we do not pause to consider the concrete intentionality of these two tablets of commandments.

II. The Human Self as Member and Failure

We may first consider the commandments negatively, suggesting that a self constituted by the habits and disciplines of amnesia, denial, autonomy, despair, and solitariness will have little energy or passion for these two defining, restraining obligations. This in Psalm 10 where the "wicked" are characterized pejoratively, it is said of them:

> For the wicked boast of the desires of their heart,
>   those greedy for gain curse and renounce the LORD.
> In the pride of their countenance the wicked say,
>   "God will not seek it out";
>   all their thoughts are, "There is no God" . . .
> They stoop, they crouch,
>   and helpless fall by their might.
> They think in their heart, "God has forgotten,
>   he has hidden his face, he will never seek it out."
>   (Ps 10:3–4, 10–11)

The motif is reiterated in Ps 73:11; Zeph 1:12; and Jer 5:12. In none of these statements is the reality of God denied. What is denied is that God has any freedom of action, having been reduced to an impotent totem. It is important to notice, in both Psalm 10 and Psalm 73, that this *bold dismissal of God* is linked to *abuse of the neighbor*:

> Their mouths are filled with cursing and deceit and oppression;
>   under their tongues are mischief and iniquity.
> They sit in ambush in the villages;
>   in hiding places they murder the innocent.
> Their eyes stealthily watch for the helpless;
>   they lurk in secret like a lion in its covert;
> they lurk that they may seize the poor;
>   they seize the poor and drag them off in their net. (Ps 10:7–10)

> Therefore pride is their necklace;
>   violence covers them like a garment . . .
> They scoff and speak with malice;
>   loftily they threaten oppression. (Ps 73:6, 8)

The tradition understands quite well that where *God is not loved*, the *neighbor will not be loved*. It is surely recognized in the tradition that where God is not present, "everything is possible," everything barbaric and anti-neighborly.

Positively, we may imagine that the covenanted self, in this tradition, is precisely nurtured in habits and disciplines that concern the concreteness of loving God and specificity of loving neighbor. Thus the large obligations of the Ten Commandments are construed, in subsequent interpretation, in more specific ways so that the self is nurtured to a ready propensity in the direction of these twin loves.

As we ponder the two "tablets" of love of God and love of neighbor, there is between the two tablets in the fourth commandment a provision for Sabbath. Sabbath rest, the regular, disciplined, public, visible cessation of "getting and spending" is a dramatic recognition that such a self inhabits (so "habits") a very different world that is not preoccupied with self-advancement or self-securing. Indeed the prophet Amos recognizes the impatience with Sabbath by those whose lives are restlessly propelled by aggressive economic activity (Amos 8:4–6). Patrick D. Miller has observed that the fourth commandment is a defining discipline for the entire Ten, because it looks back to *the rest of God* who is the focus of the first three commandments and it looks forward to *the rest of the neighbor* who is the subject of the final six commandments.[2] Thus the obligation of Sabbath encompasses all of reality, the God of heaven (see Gen 2:1–4) and the neighbor on earth (Gen 1:28–31). Sabbath is a principle habit among many habits whereby the self nurtured in covenant refuses the restless self of possessive individualism who end in either hubris or despair. In his splendid exposition of the habits and disciplines of Judaism, Michael Fishbane has seen that habits like the Sabbath generate "caesural events of godliness":

> It is thus a core task of covenant theology to live within the naturalness of our natural lives, as creatures of the earth who work and eat and labor and die—like all other living beings; but to try to turn those occasions into markers of praise and thankfulness before God, the Life of all life. Insofar as the self can stand in this conjunction, all moments enact the covenant between God's "I shall be" and the human, "We shall do and we shall hear." The routine happenings of life may thus become caesural events of godliness and the caesural may also somehow be integrated into a coherent spiritual life.[3]

The Sabbath in particular is an act of divestment from the ordinary world: "This is dying within life for love of God. It is a divestment of will for God's sake—and the wonder of the world."[4] The specific disciplines of covenantal

---

2. Miller, "The Human Sabbath," 81.
3. Fishbane, *Sacred Attunement*, 119.
4. Fishbane, *Sacred Attunement*, 128.

life are for the maintenance of "mindfulness," says Fishbane, of being a covenanted self in a world occupied by God and by neighbor who are to be loved and taken seriously. Jon Levenson, moreover, has seen that the daily performances of rituals of obedience do indeed shape the self toward faithfulness:

> It is also important to remember that, like other habitual behaviors, rituals are hardy—like habits difficult to break—and thus likely to survive the spiritual dry periods when faith and feelings are just not there . . . When the ritual is no longer observed, the likelihood that the message with which it is associated will survive, and the likelihood that old practice will come to be associated with new meanings declines still further.[5]

In an appeal to the wisdom of Rabbi Huna, Levenson concludes with a wondrous phrase:

> Torah has a power—"the starter dough that is in it"—that can transform those who study it, elevating the motivation to match the deed . . . Behaviors over time, become dispositions; observances become acts of devotion.[6]

IV.

It remains only to observe that the acquiring, maintenance, and practice of such habits and disciplines in attentiveness to Torah obedience are a *delight* and not primarily a *duty* (though it is that as well). It is a delight because obedience is a mode of communication with the God who gives commands that makes for life. Too much Christian caricature of the adherence to Torah in Judaism has concluded that Torah obedience is a compulsion of legalism or moralism. An ounce of attention to the Torah Psalms would have taught us otherwise. In Psalm 1, the introduction to the Psalter, continuing attentiveness to the Torah is a way to well-being. But it is the long Psalm 119 that bespeaks joy in such obedience, joy because one has the sense and assurance that love of God and love of neighbor constitute acts whereby we "come down where we ought to be." The psalmist knows that keeping Torah permits one to talk at liberty:

---

5. Levenson, *The Love of God*, 33
6. Levenson, *The Love of God*, 35.

Obedience

> I will keep your law continually,
>   forever and ever.
> I shall walk at liberty,
>   for I have sought your precepts . . .
> The Torah is my delight. (Ps 119: 44–45, 174)

The psalmist has clarity about Torah obedience:

> I hate the double-minded,
>   but I love your law. (v. 113)

The term "double-minded" suggests a lukewarm, half-hearted resolve that yields ambiguity. The only other use of the term is in the narrative of Elijah a Mt. Carmel where the prophets accuses his adversaries of "limping along" on two different opinions, in that case YHWH and Baal. Such double-mindedness is an attempt to have it both ways, to love God and yet avoid singular loyalty, love of neighbor and yet to seek for one's self. The habits and disciplines of Torah obedience, grounded in exodus emancipation, yield a very different way of life that precludes the despairing fatigue that comes with double-mindedness.

The wonder of Torah obedience, so well exhibited in the narrative of Moses, is that it is a genuinely dialogical transaction in which the Lord of the covenant invites and intends a) disputatious engagement with the commandments, their meaning and interpretation, and b) the on-going work of keeping such habits and disciplines contemporary to new and emerging circumstances (Exod 32–34; see Job 42:7–8). This kind of Torah obedience as dialogic engagement and unending interpretation precludes two temptations. On the one hand, it precludes *blind submissiveness* as though obedience were to a rule rather than engagement in a lively relationship. On the other hand, it precludes *wholesale resistance* to obedience as though one's self depended upon scuttling a relationship of fidelity. The two temptations are powerfully represented among us by Enlightenment emancipation on the one hand that imagines autonomy, and on the other hand a reaction to such modernist emancipation in thoughtless submissiveness to an absolute code of conduct. It is the on-going compelling act of interpretation that keeps obedience lively, pertinent, satisfying, and generative. That is why the Torah tradition, in both Judaism and Christianity, continues to engage in the work so poignantly voiced and performed by Jesus: "You have heard that it was said to those of ancient times . . . but I say to you . . ." (Matt 5:21). Jesus is giving new interpretive articulation to Torah obedience. The habits and disciplines of a covenantal life are dynamic and demanding, rooted in what is old and treasured, but kept contemporary by bold interpretation. Such an act of interpretation refuses to have human life reduced to the kind of absolute enslavements for which Pharaoh stands as a perennial symbol. It is against such enslaving absolutism that the covenanted self is addressed exactly by the God "who brought you out of the land of Egypt, out of the house of bondage" (Exod 20:1).

8

Sin

How Deep, How "Original," How Forgivable

THE COVENANTED SELF IS socialized in habits and disciplines that make an emancipated, dialogical existence possible. The form of that emancipated, dialogical existence, in the sweep of the Old Testament, is the covenant at Sinai. In that dramatic encounter, often reiterated in liturgical performance, Israel—and its members—are bound to YHWH the God of the exodus in defining ways (Exod 19–24). In that covenant-making process, Israel is assured of YHWH's fidelity. But Israel is also pledged to obedience to commandments (habits and disciplines) that give shape and structure to the relationship of fidelity.

As Israel tells and reperforms its paradigmatic narrative, that covenantal relationship is almost immediately skewed and distorted by Israel's unwillingness to practice the obedience to which it is pledged. The form of that unwillingness is narrated in the Golden Calf episode (Exod 32) whereby Israel, in its anxiety, promptly makes for itself substitute gods who displace the Lord of the covenant. That substitute God, manufactured out of gold, makes none of the *demands* of the God of Sinai, and offers none of those *assurances*. What it does do is reduce "divine power" to manageable proportion by lodging it in a manipulatable commodity (gold), albeit a precious commodity. This narrative of the Golden Calf is paradigmatic for all sin in Israel:

II. The Human Self as Member and Failure

> The LORD said to Moses, "Go down at once! Your people, whom you brought out of the land of Egypt, have acted perversely; they have been quick to turn aside from the way that I commanded them; they have cast for themselves an image of calf, and have worshiped it and sacrificed to it, and said, "These are your gods, O Israel, who brought you up out of the land of Egypt!" The LORD said to Moses, "I have seen this people, how stiff-necked they are." (Exod 32:7-9)

Karl Barth sees that the generic view of sin in Gen 3 is, in this narrative, given concrete, historical specificity:

> Here in Ex. 32 the tradition of Israel speaks from direct knowledge. Here is the setting of the view of man in relation to God which is attested in Gen. 3, being there projected backward and referred to the beginning of all peoples ... No wonder that the contours and colours of Gen. 3 seem to be mild compared with what we find here. Here it comes home with a vengeance. It is not a matter now of Adam in a distant paradise in the distant past. It is the Israelite himself now, liberated out of Egypt, brought into the wilderness, sustained in it, brought back into the land of his fathers, a member of the covenant people elected and called and infinitely preferred and therefore infinitely responsible and committed before all other peoples.[1]

The sin here is the refusal to accept the God of Sinai in all of God's majestic freedom, and the wish to generate instead a God who can be controlled: "Such was the breach of the covenant in Ex. 32—man as *creator Dei*, self-controlling and self-sufficient and self-satisfying man, the man of sin in this first from of his pride."[2]

Thus the covenant of Sinai (Exod 19–24) into which the covenantal self is socialized presses us immediately into a recognition of sin (Exod 32–34). The matter of sin, in its covenantal casting, requires careful attention because it is readily given to twin misleading judgments. On the one hand, sin is not simply ruling-breaking as though God were a score-keeper. On the other hand, sin is not a genetically transmitted disease, as it is characterized in some absolutizing articulations.

To be sure, sin is a violation of commandment. In the Golden Calf episode, it is the first two commandments of Sinai that are violated: "No other gods" and "no graven images" (Exod 20:2-6). In the subsequent prophetic

---

1. Barth, *Church Dogmatics* IV/1, 427.
2. Barth, *Church Dogmatics* IV/1, 432.

tradition, sin is most often the violation of commandments concerning the neighbor: "Do not kill, do not commit adultery, do not steal, do not bear false witness, do not covet" (Exod 20:13–17). The commands are clear, terse, and uncompromising. As we have seen in our discussion of "habits and disciplines," however, the commandments are simply modes of loyalty to YHWH. Thus in the tradition of covenant sin is not a *violation of rules*; it is a *violation of the relationship* upon which everything depends. It is an act of betrayal and infidelity against the emancipatory God who has pledged loyalty and has summoned Israel to uncompromising responsive loyalty.

It is clear in Exod 32 that the manufacture of an alternative God is a profound affront to YHWH who is provoked to anger, because such an act violates YHWH's majesty and subjects YHWH to humiliation in the eyes so the other gods: "Now let me alone, so that my wrath may burn hot against them and I may consume them; and of you I will make a great nation" (Exod 32:10).

We may consider this violation of fidelity and affront to Israel's covenantal partner by identifying two mistakes that are often made concerning sin. First, sin as rule-breaking. There is no doubt that the violation of commandments is taken seriously in the covenantal faith of Israel. Thus, for example, Hosea can convict Israel of systematically violating the commandments:

> Swearing, lying, and murder,
>   and stealing and adultery break out;
>   bloodshed follows bloodshed. (Hos 4:2)

There is no doubt, moreover, that some sins are more grievous than other sins. That is, some violations of the relationship are more offensive and disruptive than other offenses, depending upon how they demean, humiliate, or provoke the Lord of the covenant. If, however, we keep in mind that it is all about the covenantal relationship, it is clear that sins cannot be sorted out and categorized in a scholastic way as the church has long since done in terms of "venial" or "mortal" sins. Such categorization fails to take seriously the relational affective dimension of sin that violates linkage to YHWH who loves passionately and persistently, but who in freedom will not be managed by score-keeping devices. Thus before the commandments are listed in Hos 4:2, the poet speaks relationally:

> There is no faithfulness or loyalty,
>   and no knowledge of God in the land. (v. 1)

II. The Human Self as Member and Failure

The commandments are a subset of relational categories.

Second, serious consideration may be given to the popular and uncritical notion of "the fall" and the import of "original sin." It is a long-standing practice to read the violation of Adam and Eve in Gen 3 as the act whereby "sin enters the world." In later readings of the text, to be sure, that dramatic understanding of sin is fully attested. This is the case not only with Paul in his epistles who concluded that in Adam all sinned. It is also attested in Judaism of the New Testament period in the text of 2 Esdras:

> How much better it would have been if the earth had never produced Adam at all or, since it has done so, if he had been restrained from sinning! For what good does it do us all to live in misery now and have nothing but punishment to expect after death? O Adam, what have you done? Your sin was not your fall alone; it was ours also, the fall of all your descendants. What good is the promise of immortality to us, when we have committed mortal sins; or the hope of eternity, in the wretched and futile state to which we have come; or the prospect of dwelling in health and safety, when we have lived such evil lives? . . . What good is the revelation of paradise and its imperishable fruit, the source or perfect satisfaction and healing? For we shall never enter it, since we have made depravity our home. (2 Esdras 7:46–54)

This later text may reflect the influence of the early Christian tradition. It is important to appreciate the fact that such reading of the Gen 3 text is a quite late one. It is the case that in the Old Testament itself, there is no suggestion that the narrative of Gen 3 is given such an important or influential place. In the Old Testament it is the "historical" narrative of Exod 32 that articulates Israel's propensity to sin against YHWH—or alternatively it is David's violation of Uriah and Bathsheba in 2 Sam 11 that is the paradigmatic sin of ancient Israel, a violation that sets in motion the destructive power of "the sword" (2 Sam 12:9–10). It is helpful to see that in these texts of Exod 32 and 2 Sam 11 the reality of sin is said to be is a matter of choosing, and it is only later in the tradition that such "historical" choosing is "kicked upstairs" to an ontological reality.

Consequently we are able to consider the phrase "original sin" that is linked to the narrative of Gen 3. Such phrasing may suggest a genetic indictment of sin as though it were transmitted in a bodily, physical way from one generation to the next. But of course the phrase need not be taken in a genetic way. Rather it suggests "sin in principle" because the human self is understood in the biblical tradition (as Israel is understood in the prophetic tradition of the Old Testament) as inclined to distort or escape the requirements of the covenantal relationship, and so to violate the essential fidelity of healthy humanness. As the catechism of my childhood said it, "We are prone by nature to sin." That statement does not convict of sin, but acknowledges that there is a readiness or inclination to live against dialogical fidelity. That acknowledgement is a recognition that we human selves are ready and characteristically do depart from or distort dialogical fidelity, because dialogical loyalty to the God of the covenant is demanding and requires on-going attentiveness.

There are two ways to escape or distort that relationship. On the one hand, the more obvious escape or distortion is, as Karl Barth noted, to be "self-controlling and self-sufficient and self-satisfying man—the man of sin in this first form of pride."[3]

That Promethean understanding of the prideful self voiced by Karl Barth and Reinhold Niebuhr has been critiqued as a specifically "male" seduction. But the refusal of dialogic engagement can also be enacted by a blind submissiveness, a refusal to engage in dialogical contestation with God, as Moses does so vigorously. Perhaps Job's friend in the book of Job represent this refusal of such engagement, because they accept in uncritical fashion the rule-based obedience of obligation, and will explain and justify everything according to those rules. In the end, they are contrasted with the vigorous dialogical contestation of the character of Job who is commended by God for having spoken "what is right" (Job 42:7–8). What is right, in this context, is the capacity to challenge and contest God and the rule-based certitude that the friends linked to God.

Thus the escape form or distortion of that defining relationship with God may take the form of an *overstatement of self* in pride or an *understatement of self* in too-ready submissiveness. Healthy faith in the covenantal tradition is a refusal of such pride or submissiveness. In the textual tradition, we have the courageous models of Moses, the character of Job, and Jeremiah who engage in such practice; to those we may add the woman in Jesus' parable concerning prayer in which she is commended for her readiness to engage passionately and persistently with the unjust judge (Luke 18:1–8). Of the woman Jesus concludes:

> And will not God grant justice to his chosen ones who cry to him day and night? Will he delay long in helping them? I tell you, he

---

3. Barth, *Church Dogmatics* IV/1, 432.

II. The Human Self as Member and Failure

will quickly grant justice to them. And yet, when the Son of Man comes, will he find faith on earth? (vv. 7–8).

Faith, in contrast to sin, is the readiness and capacity to uphold one's side of the dialogue of fidelity and contestation. Sin is a refusal to be one's *full free self at risk* in the presence of God. We are "prone" to refuse such risk in either pride or submissiveness. The outcome of such a refusal is not, as much popular talk has it, guilt. It is rather alienation from God, out of sync with our true selves, a distortion that cuts us off from the goodness of God. That alienation, moreover, takes the form of contradiction in which we human selves are other than the selves we intend to be and are destined by God to be. We are in such a way cut off, not only from the wonder of God, but from the wonder of our true selves who are willed by God to be "lost in wonder love, and praise." We arrive at a helplessness to which the familiar "Psalm of David" gives voice:

> Against you, you alone, have I sinned,
>   and done what is evil in your sight,
> so that you are justified in your sentence
>   and blameless when you pass judgment.
> Indeed, I was born guilty,
>   a sinner when my mother conceived me. (Ps 51:4–5)

According to tradition voiced in the superscription the actual sin of David was an act of historical choosing. He, however, experiences it as a "sin in principle," as it looms in defining ways for his life with God.

II.

The wonder of that deep and honest confession of Ps 51 is that the speaker (traditionally David) who acknowledges alienation from God can turn promptly to hope-filled expectation and can address God with imperative petitions:

> Create in me a clean heart, O God,
>   and put a new and right spirit within me.
> Do not cast me away from your presence,
>   and do not take your holy spirit from me.
> Restore me to the joy of your salvation,
>   and sustain in me a willing spirit. (Ps 51:10–12)

The wonder of biblical testimony about sin is that even in such alienation, restoration is thinkable and receivable.

Thus even in the aftermath of the episode of the Gold Calf, Moses can negotiate with God (Exod 33:12–23), and finally can petition God for pardon and restoration (34:8–9). Moses knows, and the entire tradition knows, that restoration beyond alienation cannot be undertaken by alienated selves, but depends wholly upon God. Moses and the entire tradition trust, moreover, that God—beyond anger, wrath, and judgment—has a powerful yearning for and readiness to grant restoration. Thus in response to Moses' petition in Exod 34:8–9 and in the wake of the narrative of the Golden Calf, YHWH responds in readiness:

> I hereby make a covenant. Before all your people I will perform miracles such as have not been performed in all the earth, or in any nation; and people among whom you live shall see the work of the Lord; it is an awesome thing that I will do with you. (v. 10)

The ultimate truth of the Bible is that God "is more ready to give good gifts" than we to receive them. When we turn to the reality of God attested in the Bible, it is as though whatever we may think about "the fall" "original sin" or score-keeping formulae, the reality of God simply overwhelms all of our performances and stereotypes of self-destructive alienation. The church has never found a single adequate way to speak about God's capacity for fidelity beyond our refusal. As a result, the church has found useful a variety of images and metaphors for the overwhelming readiness of God. Here we may notice three of these metaphors that have exercised immense influence in the church as we recognize that each of them is not finally an adequate expression of what we know and trust:

1. The preferred usage of much of popular faith in our culture is the *priestly, ritual* rhetoric of sacrificial offering on our behalf. That language comes out of the sacrificial inventory of the book of Leviticus and is featured in the epistle to the Hebrews wherein Christ is the great High Priest who makes sacrifice, but who is also in the book of Revelation, "the lamb" who is offered as sacrifice. This rhetoric has led in popular slogans to such formulations as "substitutionary atonement" and "saved by the blood." The rhetoric appears even in more "progressive" usage as we sing:

> From heaven he came and sought her to be his holy bride,
> with his own blood he bought her, and for her life he died.[4]

4. Stone, "The Church's One Foundation."

II. The Human Self as Member and Failure

While the language is satisfying to many people, it has also degenerated into a sort of magical performance in which the performance itself is effective without any personal engagement.

2. Clearly related to that rhetoric is *economic imagery* in which we have rhetoric of "redemption" whereby the "redeemer" "pays the price" of buying freedom for the sinner who is in hock to sin. The language derives from the emancipation of the exodus imagery in which YHWH "ransomed" Israel from Pharaoh by paying the debt owed by the peasant-slaves to Pharaoh:

> For I am the LORD your God,
>   the Holy One of Israel, your Savior.
> I give Egypt as your *ransom*,
>   Ethiopia and Seba in exchange for you.
>   (Isa 43:3; see Mark 10:45)

The economic imagery of "satisfying a debt" is closely linked to satisfying or "appeasing" God by paying the price, in a sacrifice of blood, but it is at root a quite different field of images.

3. A third distinct usage is *juridical*, featured especially in Paul's rhetoric of "justification by faith." In this imagery the alienated sinner stands before the judge; the judge, against compelling evidence, renders a verdict of acquittal and so pardons the affront.

There is reason that the church, informed by the biblical tradition, must appeal to and rely on many images concerning the mystery of God's transformation of the status of *the alienated* for the sake of *the relationship*, because that act it is an act that defies all of our language and our logic. Thus we must recognize a) that all of these ways of speaking about restoration are *metaphorical*, b) that each of these usages is *satisfying* to some in the community, and c) that each of these usages is *inadequate* to voice the generous mystery of God.

III.

Beyond the utilization of such images that are finally judged to be without compelling edge, the rhetoric of praise and petition in the Bible engages a cluster of terms to articulate YHWH's ready capacity for restorative relationship. In this vocabulary there is no longer focus on a refusal or distortion of dialogic engagement; there is only glad concentration on the wonder of God. That vocabulary is featured in the stunning reversal of

Hos 2:14–15. After the effective alienation of divorce in vv. 2–13 (again a metaphor), YHWH without explanation reverses field and reembraces Israel with an overwhelming assertion of fidelity:

> And I take you for my wife forever; I will take you for my wife in righteousness and in justice, in steadfast love, and in mercy. I will take you for my wife in faithfulness, and you shall know the LORD.

The same rhetoric is employed in Israel's praise that celebrates YHWH's generativity that reaches endlessly beyond "our iniquities":

> The LORD is merciful and gracious,
>   slow to anger and abounding in steadfast love.
> He will not always accuse,
>   nor will he keep his anger forever.
> He does not deal with us according to our iniquities,
>   nor repay us according to our iniquities. (Ps 103:8–10)

In Israel's practice of urgent petition, moreover, the same vocabulary becomes the ground for hope-filled prayer:

> But you, O LORD, are a God merciful and gracious,
>   slow to anger and abounding in steadfast love and faithfulness.
> Turn to me and be gracious to me;
>   give your strength to your servant,
>   save the child of your serving girl.
> Show me a sign of your favor . . .
>   because you, LORD, have helped me and comforted me.
> (Ps 86:15–17)

This reiterated rhetoric arises in the orbit of family concerning husband and wife or parent and child. Its usage, however, is not limited to such specific reference, but becomes Israel's most familiar, most treasured, and deepest articulation of new possibility from God in the face of alienation.

In the wake of the Golden Calf narrative, moreover, in the renewed negotiation between YHWH and Moses, YHWH will employ two of the term from this vocabulary to voice YHWH's ready generous freedom: "I will be gracious to whom I will be gracious, and I will show mercy on whom I will show mercy" (Exod 33:19). And in follow-up, as a ground for Moses' confession and petition, YHWH can declare of YHWH's self:

> The LORD, the LORD,
>   a God merciful and gracious, slow to anger,
>   and abounding in steadfast love and faithfulness,

II. The Human Self as Member and Failure

> Keeping steadfast love for the thousandth generation,
> forgiving iniquity and transgression and sin ... (Exod 34:6–7)

The outcome of this extravagant language of generous fidelity is that Israel, beyond its alienation—in narrative (Exod 34), oracle (Hos 2), doxology (Ps 103), and complaint (Ps 86)—found a way to look forward to the new initiative of YHWH that would permit new community, new selves in that community, and new historical possibility. There is no looking back. There is no brooding about a failed past. There is only joyous anticipation of new life grounded in divine generosity. The tradition does not linger over past negations, but instead focuses on the newness performed and empowered by divine generosity.

That new community and new selves within the community now face into the future unencumbered. Thus Jeremiah can anticipate that the Torah will be "written on their hearts" for ready, glad obedience (Jer 31:33). Ezekiel anticipates a new heart of flesh ready for obedience:

> A new heart I will give you, and new spirit I will put within you; and I will remove from your body the heart of stone and give you a heart of flesh. AI will put my spirit within you, and make you follow my statutes and be careful to observe my ordinances. (Ezek 36:26–27)

Isaiah can imagine new "oaks of righteousness" that will repair the wounded city:

> to give them garland instead of ashes,
> the oil of gladness instead of mourning,
>   the mantle of praise instead of a fainting spirit.
> They will be called oaks of righteousness,
>   the planting of the LORD, to display his glory.
> They shall build up the ancient ruins,
>   they shall raise up the former devastations;
> they shall repair the ruined cities,
>   the devastations of many generations. (Isa 61:3–4)

The alienation is overcome; the contradiction is nullified. Covenanted selves, with glad embrace of habits and disciplines of deep fidelity, are on their way rejoicing!

9

Racism Right from Our Earliest Texts

THE BIBLE IS NOT preoccupied with racial questions. It is, however, preoccupied with "chosen peoples," Israel in the Old Testament and the church in the New Testament. The notion of "chosen people" inevitably elevates one population to a state of preference and so casts other peoples as less important, less valued, and less entitled, and less beloved. It is easy enough to transpose that casting of "chosenness" into a question of race, because "racial" differentiation is the process of regarding one people as more important, more valued, more entitled, and more beloved than another. In what follows I will consider four biblical texts in which such "chosenness" works to the devaluing of "the other." I will in each case match that claim of chosenness with a way whereby such chosenness can be and is countered in a rethink that refuses conventional conclusions of chosenness.

I.

In the book of Genesis, Joseph, his father Jacob, and his several brothers travel to Egypt because there is a famine in their homeland. Pharaoh, the great accumulator and monopolizer, welcomes them. All goes well until they are ready to eat. But then, we are told, there are rules against Egyptians eating with "Hebrews." "Hebrews" (as distinct from Israelites or later Jews) are low-class people at the bottom of the economic order and of the food chain. Obviously Pharaoh and his entourage dominate the food chain. That difference is sufficient ground for the verdict that they cannot eat together:

> They served him [Joseph] by himself, and the Egyptians who ate with him by themselves, because the Egyptians could not eat with the Hebrews, for that is an *abomination* to the Egyptians. (Gen 43:32)

What caught my eye was the term "abomination." We do not expect that term here, because it means "deeply objectionable and disgusting." The Hebrews are deeply objectionable and disgusting to the Egyptians, and nothing is more deeply objectionable and disgusting than eating with such people. (Memories of the "lunch counters"!)

We are not told what the objection to the Hebrews is, but we can track the term "abomination" in two other uses in this narrative. In Gen 46:33–34 it is reported that "all shepherds" are an abomination to the Egyptians:

> When Pharaoh calls you and says, "What is your occupation?" you shall say, "Your servants have been keepers of livestock from our youth even until now, both we and our ancestors"—in order that you may settle in the land of Goshen, because all shepherds are *abhorrent* [abomination] to the Egyptians.

Shepherds were outside the demand economy of Pharaoh, slightly beyond administrative control, and likely not very clean and not very cultured. They are dismissed wholesale as an occupational group. The third use of our term is in the report that Israelite worship (sacrifices) are an *abomination* to Egyptians, perhaps because those sacrifices are addressed to a strange emancipatory God who jeopardized Pharaoh's world and his control of the economy, or perhaps because they engaged in religious practices different from Egyptians practices. We know that folk down the socio-economic ladder often engage in more emotional religious exercises that appear to be "out of control" (Exod 8:26; the NRSV translates as "offensive").

The term "abomination" functions to establish and assert the superiority of the Egyptians and the profound inferiority of the Hebrews who were *not welcome at the table*, who had *low-grade occupations*, and who engaged in *objectionable worship*. It is a triad of socializing (eating), economic activity (shepherding), and worship, a triad that encompasses most of public life. It is telling that in none of these references are we told why or in what ways they are an abomination. It is rather an "understood" and tacit fact in the dominant community.

The narrative of Genesis–Exodus shows what happens to a people that is labeled an "abomination." First they are subjected to "purity codes" that protect the code-managers and exclude all others. Thus "abomination" figures in the purity codes of the book of Leviticus, and in white society that by its purity codes has long excluded non-whites from food, from schools, from economic opportunity and jobs.

The justifying force of purity codes makes the objectionable people economically vulnerable and dependent. We are told in Gen 47:13–25 that the peasant community, surely including the Hebrews, was reduced into debt and economic dependence. It does not surprise us that the purity codes and resultant economic pressure on the vulnerable excluded reduce them to slavery through unpayable debts. Thus the outcome from such social distinctions ends with cheap labor for Pharaoh who are without rights and who can be treated in exploitative ways in the service of the surplus wealth of Pharaoh (see Exod 1:8–14)

It is plausible that this Pharaonic narrative is not rooted in historical specificity. Rather it is a paradigmatic text that is in practice reperformed over and over as a distinct "class" of people employs purity codes and their spin-off in economic matters to create a dependent "class" of cheap labor that is locked hopelessly in debt. The narrative knows how the world works! It requires no imagination at all to see that this narrative is reperformed many times and in our own contemporary society.

Thus it is easy to see our purity codes in US society have excluded (segregated) Blacks from every kind of socio-economic possibility and have tied that exclusionary practice to religious validation as whites of European extraction are seen and said to be superior to others who could not, until recent time, eat with the whites. The current hysteria concerning "immigration" is only the most recent replication of this model narrative in which immigrants from "elsewhere" are demonized and dismissed as "unworthy" and unqualified for membership in "our" society.

That much of this ancient narrative is not surprising. It is quite familiar in our own social experience. What surprises is that the biblical narrative, and the God of the biblical narrative, will not accept this status quo of Pharaoh as the wave of the future. The exodus narrative is an account of how the dynamic processes of history, propelled by the God of emancipation, causes the tables (sic: the tables for eating!) to be turned on the "master race" of Pharaoh. In the face of Pharaoh, it is asserted that this company of soon-to-be-emancipated slaves is indeed "God's first-born son" (Exod 4:22), and as first-born son comes with great entitlement. The exodus consists in mobilizing this "mixed multitude" of nobodies (Exod 12:38) so that by the resolve of God they become God's "treasured possession out of all the peoples," "a priestly kingdom and a holy nation" (Exod 19:5–6). It turns out that the categories of "unclean and impure" whereby some are excluded from economic viability and social participation are in the end unsustainable!

There is a parallel restlessness in our US society as the old white privileged power structure, sustained by purity codes, is in deep jeopardy, as more and more non-whites find their voice and refuse any longer to be denied access and entitlement by legal labeling supported by purity codes. Much of the agitation for the recovery of old economic arrangements, coupled in many instances with convenient religious slogans, concerns the loss of privilege, the end of a cheap labor supply that could only be sustained by a tacit consensus on ritual exclusion.

II.

It took a very long time for the marginated Hebrews, marked as a "mixed multitude" and emancipated by God, to become an actual historical embodiment of "chosenness." But it did happen via David and Solomon and the Jerusalem establishment with its temple priests and scribes. The community of covenant imagined at Sinai to be a "holy people" eventually became quite intentional and self-conscious about its chosenness, to the exclusion of the non-chosen.

Specifically when the elite Israelites in Jerusalem were deported by the Babylonians into a "foreign land" (see Ps 137), and eventually were permitted by the Persians to return home (see 2 Chr 36:22–23), their status as chosen took on enormous power. Over time this deeply chosen community of elites developed a "Holiness Code" (in the book of Leviticus) that consisted in rules of purity and cleanness that served directly to exclude all those who did not "qualify" and meet requirements. The book of Deuteronomy, the master script for covenantal identity, affirmed Israel as the chosen people of YHWH (Deut 14:1–2) and offered a detailed inventory of foods that would be "abhorrent" (abomination) that must be avoided in order to maintain holiness (14:3–21). Beyond that, the same text offered an inventory of those peoples who were to be perpetually precluded from the assembly of YHWH:

> No Ammonite or Moabite shall be admitted to the assembly of the Lord. Even to the tenth generation none of their descendants shall be admitted to the assembly of the Lord, because they did

not meet you with food and water in your journey out of Egypt and because they hired against you Balaam son of Beor, from the Pethor of Mesopotamia, to curse you. Yet the LORD your God refused to heed Balaam; the LORD your God turned the curse into a blessing for you. You shall never promote their welfare or their prosperity as long as you live. (Deut 23:3–6)

The matter of exclusion came to a head in the later fifth century when the scribe Ezra was leading the surviving elite remnant of deportees back to Jerusalem at the permit of the Persian Empire. In a quite remarkable report to Ezra, we learn that the community of the elite remnant is in crisis:

After these things had been done, the officials approached me and said, "The people of Israel, the priests and the Levites have not separated themselves from the peoples of the land with their abominations, from the Canaanites, the Hittites, the Perizzites, the Jebusites, the Ammonites, the Moabites, the Egyptians, and the Amorites. For they have taken some of their daughters for wives for themselves and their sons. Thus the holy seed has mixed itself with the peoples of the land, and in this faithlessness the officials and leader have led the way." (Ezra 9:1–2)

There had been intermarriage with other peoples. The key assertion is that the "holy seed" (semen) is compromised. Ezra responds to the report with high indignation: "When I heard this, I tore my garment and my mantle, and pulled hair from my head and beard, and sat appalled" (v. 3).

Intermarriage always compromises the superiority of the supervising community. The defiant act of intermarriage is not unlike the violation of that same racial taboo in our society for a very long time. That provision of intermarriage among us was of course hypocritical; while the facade of racial purity was maintained, ample evidence shows that white power exercised in covert unequal relationships was permitted and accepted, as long as the appearance of piety and propriety were intact.

The administration of purity by Ezra suggests what a powerful force such notions of racial purity can take on. Ezra and Nehemiah were charged, they assumed, with the maintenance of the "holy seed." They took the drastic step of terminating "mixed marriages" that violate purity, and sent the Gentile wives home and away from Israel (Neh 13:23–27). This action of Ezra in maintaining racial ethnic purity is perfect counterpoint to the similar action we have seen taken at the outset by Pharaoh in the expulsion of the Hebrews from his table. While the action of Ezra is more radical to be sure, the social effect is parallel. Both Pharaoh and Ezra are propelled by a religious conviction that has immense economic implications. Indeed, Samuel Adams has proposed that the break-up of such marriages to "foreign women" intended to keep family estates from falling into the hands of "outsiders":

> Ezra's reading of the legal sources seems to reflect an exclusivist party, and one of the motivations for their rigid viewpoint is tight control of ancestral property rights . . . The decision by such persons to intermarry would have meant potential forfeiture of property to outsiders, especially those who did not go into exile . . .This verse [10:8] indicates that Ezra's rigid opposition to intermarriage represents the best means for the exilic community to maintain property for themselves.[1]

Yet again the hidden connection between religious purity and economic advantage is just below the surface of the text.

But of course, post-exilic Judaism did not readily settle in such an exclusionary posture. We can find evidence against such a tight notion of chosenness. Isaiah 56 is a spectacular instance of an alternative to Ezra's program. That particular text provides for the welcome of foreigners and eunuchs into the assembly of Judaism, two populations excluded in the old inventory of Deut 23. This text makes explicit provision for the inclusion of these "objectionable types." Concerning eunuchs (on which see Deut 23:1):

> To the eunuchs who keep my sabbaths,
>   who choose the things that please me
>   and hold fast my covenant,
> I will give, in my house and within my walls,
>   a monument and a name,
>   better than sons and daughters;
> I will give them an everlasting name
>   that shall not be cut off. (Isa 56:4–5)

Concerning foreigners in vv. 6–7a:

> And the foreigners who join themselves to the LORD,
>   to minister to him, to love the name of the LORD,
>   and to be his servants,
>   all who keep sabbath, and do not profane it,
>   and hold fast my covenant—

---

1. Adams, *Social and Economic Life in Second Temple Judea*, 26–27.

> these I will bring to my holy mountain,
> and make them joyful in my house of prayer . . .

The welcome for such "unclean" types is voiced in the wondrous conclusion of v. 7:

> These I will bring to my holy mountain,
> and make joyful in my house of prayer;
> their burnt offerings and their sacrifices
> will be accepted on my altar;
> for my house shall be called a house of prayer
> for all peoples.

All are welcome! This would seem to be a decisive challenge to Ezra's policy. Isaiah declares that the holiness provisions to exclude the "impure" are null and void. So in our society, a series of court decisions has been required to break the lawful practice of exclusion. But of course court decisions can only address the law. They cannot address the religious underpinning of racial exclusion that features both long-standing traditional practice and contemporary anxiety in most acute forms. So now, the presence of "foreigners" in the US (that characteristically, specifically refers to people who are not of European extraction) is seen as a disruption of a God-given destiny as the leader of the pure white world. This urgent advocacy for such holiness-cum-entitlement is simply a contemporary echo of the old mantras of chosenness.

III.

The matter of holiness, purity, and exclusion turned out to be no less acute in the New Testament. In the Gospel of Mark, Jesus has just delivered an instruction about purity and defilement, and insists that it is conduct and not "things" that defile (Mark 7:1–23). But then in the next paragraph he is confronted by a Gentile woman whose daughter has an "unclean" spirit (Mark 7:24–30). The woman, nameless and identified only by her ethnic group, asks Jesus to cast out the unclean demon, but he declares that his ministry is to "the children" (Jews) and not "the dogs" (Gentiles). That is, for all his instruction about defilement, Jesus remains committed to the notion that his work is with Jews, that is, with the chosen, well-beloved people of God. The Gospel writers are not agreed on whether he refused the woman or whether he simply gave priority in his ministry to Jews. Either way, he makes a radical racial-ethnic distinction on behalf of Jews. The woman, however, persists and instructs Jesus in a way that calls him out of his uncritical assumption about the privilege and preference of his people. It is a dramatic moment in which the old assumptions are broken by a voice of insistence from outside the matrix of privilege and superiority.

It is remarkable that in the sequence of the Markan narrative that just before this encounter, Jesus has performed a "feeding miracle" in Galilee, that is, for Jews (Mark 6:30–44). And just after this encounter he performs a "feeding miracle" in the Decapolis, that is, for Gentiles (Mark 8:1–10). It is as though in this dramatic moment he has gotten the point from the woman and promptly acts on it. He moves out of the safe cocoon of chosenness to acknowledge in a concrete way the legitimacy of "the other" in his ministry.

IV.

The struggle to include Gentiles (people outside the purity codes) in the ministry of Jesus and in the life of the church was a highly contested matter. Thus it is legitimate to move from the Gospel narrative of Mark 7 to the remarkable narrative of Peter's trance in Acts 10. In his vision he is commanded by "a voice" to eat "four-footed creatures and reptiles and birds of the air" (Acts 10:12). This is an inventory of "unclean" food to which Peter strenuously objects: "By no means Lord; for I have never eaten anything that is profane or unclean" (v. 14). Peter is being called to violate the purity code that he has trusted forever, a code that was designed to maintain the purity, the chosenness, and the preferential privilege of Jews in the sight of God. But the commanding voiced that addresses him is insistent: "What God has made clean, you must not call profane" (v. 15). After a reiteration of this exchange three times, it is not easy for Peter, but he gets it. The drama was only about unclean food. Peter, however, is quite able to extrapolate from the drama of food to broader social practice. He explains to his visitors from Joppa what the drama of his trance means: "You yourself know that it is unlawful for a Jew to associate with or to visit a Gentile; but God has shown me that I should not call anyone profane or unclean" (v. 28).

He first acknowledges the traditional teaching of his people that was based on exclusion. But then he promptly states what God has shown him in this moment of radical disclosure. What God has shown him is that the old purity distinctions are passé. What God has taught him is that purity codes and the economic leverage they carry no longer pertain. I would like to say that "the rest is history," and that the church has understood since then that the Gospel is not exclusionary. But of course history tells otherwise. The church has always again been summoned out beyond its fearful treasured chosenness, so that this is an embrace of all "peoples, tongues, and races," because, as Peter attests, "God shows no partiality" (v. 34).

V.

The matter of "race" is endlessly contested because there is so much at stake in the matter socially, ritually, and economically. In each case I have cited, the textual tradition itself protests such exclusionary conviction and practice:

—Pharaoh's failure to admit Hebrews to his table is *answered* by the exodus in which a "mixed multitude" is transposed into God's "first born."

—Ezra's exclusionary protection of "holy seed" is *contradicted* by Isaiah's vision of a house of prayer "for all peoples."

—Jesus' readiness to privilege Jess in his ministry is *contested* by the instruction of the Gentile woman.

—Peter's adherence to old purity codes is *corrected* by the voice of heaven.

Our own social contestation over inclusion and exclusion simply continues that ancient life-or-death contest. Chosenness as privilege and entitlement is vigorously alive and well among us. The matter of chosenness as racism, entitlement, and privilege is not a churchy or parochial agenda, but a matter of public health and historical possibility. The performance of race is clearly obvious in two social issues now before us. Concerning immigration the rhetoric of "alien" suggests that the "master race" is in jeopardy from lesser peoples who insists on receiving "crumbs" from the table of abundance. Concerning police power, it a sorry truth that police in our society are placed in the intolerable role of the old "drivers" of the plantation economy whose work was to keep cheap labor at work, in place, and in order. But of course all of the exclusionary rhetoric concerning both of these issues, immigration and police power—with its high claims of "Americanism" and appeal to distorted notions of the gospel—fails to reckon with the fact that both the US Constitution and the Christian Gospel tell against such fearful privilege for some at the expense of others. Ta-Nahisi

II. The Human Self as Member and Failure

Coates has made clear enough that racism is not just an idea. It is about the control of bodies, control of the political processes and of economic engines of prosperity.[2] Religious rhetoric in the service of such control is never innocent. It is, in my judgment, crucial to expose the hidden connections between *religious rhetoric of chosenness, economic advantage,* and *political domination.* The bodily reality of racism has been evident since the first Hebrew slaves "groaned and cried out" in their suffering (Exod 2:23). That suffering of the slaves began with the linkage between them and the category of "abomination." The God of emancipation intended that human bodies be accorded respect and security in a way that overrides all sense of "abomination."

---

2. Coates, *Between the World and Me.*

III

The Riddle of Silence and Speech

10

On Liturgical Silence

But the LORD is in his holy temple;
    let all the earth keep silence before him! (Hab 2:20)

THE POETRY OF HABAKKUK is commonly dated to the final decades of the Davidic dynasty in the time before the destruction of ancient Jerusalem. The poetry voices, along with a vigorous affirmation of hope at the end (Hab 3:16–19), the usual cadences of prophetic indictment and judgment. These are articulated in quite intensified rhetoric that anticipates the coming destruction of the royal city.

I.

Our familiar verse in 2:20 is a pivotal transition that is situated between two powerful poetic riffs. Just before this verse we get a series of prophetic utterances that begin with "woe" or "alas," that are commonly termed "woe oracles" (2:6–19). That introductory word bespeaks anticipated sadness and grief for big trouble that is sure to come. This series of five "woes" anticipates big trouble to come for Jerusalem because of its offensive misconduct that violates the intention of God (2:6, 9, 12 15, 19). While the anticipated big trouble to come is evoked, in prophetic horizon, because of a systemic contradiction of God's purposes, there is in fact no active intervention by

God in the purview of the poetry. The coming trouble is the inescapable outcome of misconduct, the inevitable consequence of misdeeds that violate God's ordering of creation.

Each of the five "woe oracles" in the series is expanded from the initial terse verdict governed, in our translation, by "alas." The misconduct from which will come trouble includes:

—"Heaping up what is not your own," that is, predatory coveting (2:6).

—"Evil gain for your house," that is, violent economic exploitation (v. 9).

—"Building a town with bloodshed and iniquity" (v. 12). These terms likely refer in context to exploitative labor practices and cheap wages for workers.

—"Making your neighbor drink," that is, the deliberate erosion of societal restraint in a spree of self-indulgence that makes the vulnerable even more vulnerable (v. 15).

—Worship idols of wood, stone, gold, and silver, objects that have no "breath," no life-giving capacity (v. 19).

The tone of these "woe oracles" in this extended articulation concerns a disordered society that lives at the edge of predatory violence in which neighborly possibility is precluded. It is likely that this sequence of "woe oracles" deliberately builds toward the final "woe" concerning idolatry. That is, this series of identified distorted conducts eventuates in idolatry or, alternatively, such misconduct is evidence of a disordered society that is premised on false gods who cannot give life. The outcome of the worship of false gods is endless anxiety that takes the form of anti-neighborliness. Such idolatry requires the production of safety and happiness for one's self without any gifts from elsewhere, for idols cannot give gifts.

The sum of these "woe oracles" constitutes a prophetic sketch of a society that has lost all possible grounds for a viable future. Thus the series of "woe oracles" culminates like a thud in our verse, 2:20.

II.

Our verse 2:20 is followed in 3:1–16 by a vision or anticipation of the dramatic, explosive coming of God to save "your people . . . your anointed" (3:13). This anticipation is followed in 3:17–19 by a voicing of tenacious confidence in YHWH as savior even in spite of all the evidence to the contrary.

It is certain that this narrative of theophany in 3:1–16 had no original connection to the preceding verses, but has been placed there in the wisdom of the traditioning process. This poem begins in 3:2 with a petition that God would "revive" God's saving work as in the days of old. And then in vv. 3ff. we get a description of God's remembered activity when God came in powerful ways to rescue Israel. That remembered divine coming was an exhibit of immense and dramatic power when God came from "Teman," that is, from the south, a hoary remote inaccessible mountain or desert of God's dwelling place. God came with threats and disturbances of cosmic proportion that addressed many peoples who were the enemies of God's people, thereby presenting God as the decisive ally on behalf of God's people. In this forceful poetry we get a mix of cosmic disturbance (mountains, wager, sea, moon, sun, lightning) and the military imagery of horses, chariots, and arrows. The rhetoric is super-charged with irresistible power. That power to save is like a "whirlwind" (v. 14), or takes the form of chaotic waters that the enemy cannot possibly resist (v. 15).

The intent of the entire dramatic performance is on behalf of God's people, Israel, who were saved from the wicked nations in the past and here anticipate such rescue once again, this time in the context of Babylon. The rhetoric is designed to assert a saving power from YHWH that is stronger than the mighty force of Babylon. The poem is framed at the outset by "awe" at the remembered actions of YHWH (3:2), and at the conclusion by a confident "waiting quietly" (without anxiety) for God to act again as in the past (3:16). It is this "waiting quietly" (literally "being at rest"), that is, not trying save self, that leads to *the three-fold "though"* of v. 17, then to *the formidable "yet"* of v. 18 that refuses to submit to hopeless circumstance, and finally to *the bold doxology* of v. 19. The initial "awe" of v. 2 and the concluding confidence of vv. 16–19 depend upon and are authorized by the remembered (and anticipated) coming of God in vv. 3–15. In this "coming of God" God in awesome and dramatic power has in time past and will again in time to come reverse the course of history away from misery and defeat to wellbeing for God's people. The God trusted and expected on the basis memory is not in thrall to circumstance, not intimidated by the enemy nations and their gods, but will, soon or late, override those circumstances for the sake of Israel's wellbeing.

III.

Our verse 2:20 is situated at the pivot point between the "woe oracles" (2:6–19) that anticipate the merited demise of God's people, and the anticipated revival of God's people (3:1–19), a hope rooted in God's expected decisive, irresistible reentry into the cosmic-historical process. Thus in 2:6–19 and 3:1–19 we have the two primary prophetic accents of *divine judgment* and *divine possibility*.

In our verse we look back, on the one hand, to the "woe oracles" and particularly to the final "woe" concerning idolatry (2:18–19). There is no doubt that this final "woe" concerning false worship is the deliberate climax of the series of "woes." Worship as trust in and obedience to inanimate commodities assures that there is on offer no power to save.

Our verse 2:20 thus intends a dramatic contrast between the idols who cannot save because they have no *ruah* and YHWH who is known to have ample power to save. The complete contrast between idols and YHWH is that YHWH evokes respect, awe, and silence, whereas the idols can command no respect, generate no awe, and therefore merit no awed silence. Thus the very presence of YHWH stands in complete contrast to the cheapening and trivialization of life that has been voiced in the series of "woe oracles." Our verse intends that we be caught up short and jerked out of the narcotic of self-preoccupation and self-indulgence evidenced in the "woes." The conduct featured in the "woes" had assumed, in either pride or in desperation, human autonomy wherein we are on our own and are free to do whatever we want, no matter how damaging it may be to the social infrastructure. Thus a life of disconnected autonomy without accountability permits predatory coveting, economic violence, cheap exploitative labor practices, anti-social self-indulgence, and excessive trust in commodities. And then, abruptly, this illusionary failed world is interrupted by the acknowledgement of the one who evokes awe and respect, who stands apart from and over against all such shoddy human practices. The sharp "keep silent" may have the tone of an imperative: Stop such foolish self-preoccupations that contradict reality and notice this "Other" out beyond you.

On the other hand, our verse looks forward to the anticipated dramatic intervention of Hab 3. In light of chapter 3, to which it is belatedly connected, we are invited to reflect on "his holy temple" which YHWH occupies. At first glance this may be the Jerusalem temple over which the priests serenely preside. But because the vision of God's coming testifies to a God who is not enmeshed in present circumstance, it may preferable that "his holy temple" be understood as a temple in heaven where the gods dwell, a vision that is uncompromised by any human trivialization. Or perhaps the poetry is willfully ambiguous enough that all at once "his holy temple" may be *the Jerusalem temple, the heavenly temple,* and *the remote mountain or desert habitat* from which God comes. The effect of this multiple possibility is the insistence that the God who authorizes the "woe oracles" is beyond easy human liturgical reach and will be neither captured within nor domesticated by the religious seduction of idols that constitute no threat or alternative to the holiness of God. That God's habitat is "holy" means that it must be beyond comfort zone of intimacy and easy friendship. This is a God not easily approached who for that reason evokes silent awe, respect, and submission. Such a tone evokes the probe of Jeremiah:

> Am I a God near by, says the LORD, and not a God far off?
> (Jer 23:23)

As Israel knows in the intimate psalms, this is a God who is "near"; (see Deut 4:7).[1] But this same God is "far off" and "fills heaven and earth" (Jer 23:24), and will not be presumed upon. This God occupies all of reality and will not be slotted in safe places. This affirmation is, in short, a direct contradiction of all consumer religion with its passionate pursuit of commodities (so "wood, stone, gold, silver") that regularly reduces the holiness of God down to manageable proportion, a god who asks nothing and permits everything. By contrast the God who occupies holiness evokes awe and respect, and thus sub missive silence (see Zeph 1:7 as well).

Such a rendering of God has compelling implications for liturgy that tells against every vacuous "praise hymn" and every comfortable easy prayer that presumes casual companionship and accessible familiarity that takes the form of pop entertainment, or every ideological passion that readily assumes God is "on our side." This is a presence, so the temple priests assert in our verse, that evokes awe beyond comfort and easy satisfaction, dignity that requires self-respect, and submissiveness that is not groveling but honest in the embrace of our true status. The gravitas of our verse is a declaration that life is ordered on terms other than our own. In that moment we stand alongside "all the earth," all the neighboring nations, friend and foe, all the threatening others, all the non-human creatures. We

---

1. More than anyone I know, Patrick Miller has focused on and appreciated the affirmation of "a God so near" in Deut 4:7. See both Miller, *They Cried to the Lord*, and the Festschrift in his honor: Strawn and Bowen, eds., *A God So Near: Essays on Old Testament Theology in Honor of Patrick D. Miller*.

are all together on the side of awe before the holy one. In that awe before holiness we are made mindful of our commonality with all creatures, all of whom stand together in acknowledgment of the Lord of the temple who is wholly unlike any of us. Marvin Sweeney avers that the silence "conveys the 'otherness' of holy divine speech by the angels who praise YHWH in the heavens."[2] In that silence we may inexplicably come to notice that the foregoing behavior, predatory coveting, economic violence, exploitative labor practice, unrestrained self-indulgence, and idolatry in imagined world of autonomy, is inadmissible. Thus the glad defiance of 3:17 stands in contrast to the frivolous activity castigated in the "woe oracles." In the moment of silence before holiness the contrast is seen to be complete. The whole earth in that instant knows better![3]

IV.

I will now, however, file a puckish dissent from that more-or-less conventional reading of our verse. The verse may be taken, against any magisterial theological claim, as no more than a rule for conduct in liturgy. As such it would have been enunciated by priests who presided over the temple. It must be remembered, moreover, that temples were characteristically designed by and for the king in order to serve state interests. This was surely the case in the Jerusalem temple; the city of Jerusalem itself was from the outset "the city of David" and the temple served the king in the city. The king, according to conventional politics, was in fact the chief priest. And the performing priests were in service as surrogates for the king; their work was to advance and protect royal interests. The priests were characteristically champions and administrators of royal order.

Given that political reality we may entertain the thought that our verse commending liturgical silence need not be taken at face value in theological innocence. Rather the commended silence could in reality be designed to assure *mono-vocal worship* and *mono-dimensional theological imagination* so that no voice except the voice of authorized power could be sounded, and no matter of critical substance could be imagined outside of royal-priestly-temple enterprise. Then the liturgical imagination issued in mono-voice intended to be all- comprehensive so as to contain all imaginable possibility. In such a context, other voices, notably voices of

2. Sweeney, *The Twelve Prophets*, vol. 2, 478
3. Knohl, *The Sanctuary of Silence*, 48–152.

protest that might sound grievance or voices of energy that might imagine alternative possibility, would have been heard as a challenge if not a threat to singular control that seeks to put authority beyond challenge. Such a way of silence in worship is roundly contradicted by invitations to "clap your hands" (Pss 47:1; 98:8) and "make a joyful noise to the Lord" (Ps 100:1), not even to speak of the voicing of grief before God as social grievance that confronts established order. Thus liturgical silence can be an enterprise that serves to assure the maintenance established status quo order from which the priests, among others, benefitted. It might be judged that silence is a more appropriate response to the idols in 2:18–19 than it is to the lively God of v. 20 who elsewhere mostly invites dialogic engagement.

It is easy enough for priests who operate the liturgy to confuse their liturgic investment and their political advantage with the will of God. (We professional religionists do it all the time!) In an acute critique of Christian sacramental confusion, Regina Schwartz observes the way in which the "instrumentality" of the church served "the sacramentality" (*mysterion*) of the Eucharist. That is *corpus Christi* served the *corpus mysticum*. Over time, however, matters were confused or even reversed so that the *instrumentality* of the Eucharist came to serve the *sacramentality* of the priesthood:

> The church, eager to assert the real presence of the human and the divine Christ against spiritualizing challenges, began to refer to the host as the *corpus Christi*, the body of Christ. That is, the term that originally signified the Christian Church then began to designate the consecrated host, and vice versa: the term used for the *corpus mysticum* was gradually transferred to the Church. This process was codified when Boniface VIII in 1303 issued the bull *Unam sanctum* to remind political entities that they functioned not independently but within the body of the Church . . . The Eucharist became a miracle made possible through the power of the Church—a power seemingly prior to the miracle. In this way, the Eucharist became a locus where the Church could exercise its control over the sacred.[4]

It is not difficult to imagine that the same confusion and inversion may have happened over time in the Jerusalem temple. A consequence of that inversion could have been the unchallengeable authority of the king (via the priests), an authority that was to be honored in silence without dissent, protest, or a "discouraging word." Given this possible trajectory of

---

4. Schwartz, *Sacramental Poetics at the Dawn of Secularism*, 19–20.

power and authority, one can notice how the verse lives in tension with the mention of idols (vv. 18–19) who in fact were silencers because they have no energy to evoke voice, and how our verse lives in tension as well with the theophany that follows in 3:13–15 that features a God whom it is difficult to imagine in silence. In this reading the priests who offered 2:20 confused the settled protected order of the realm with the awe evoke by God.

This dissenting possibility concerning our verse invites us, at the least, to be continually suspicious of ecclesial stifling (or socio-political stifling as in voter repression), in order to adjudicate when or if it serves the wonder of God and when or if it serves the official functionaries who have a stake in mono-vocal worship or mono-vocal politics and who may, knowingly or unwittingly, be the official silencers. At least in many other contexts, if not here, the liturgical tradition suggests that God is pleased, "magnified," and enthroned (see Ps 22:6) by loud or even boisterous affirmation and petition. "Awe" might lead to silence; or it might lead alternatively to *honesty via grievance* of *gladness via doxology*, either of which breaks the silence by such utterance. Either way, in grief or gladness, it is a dialogic alternative to the kind of silence that may only disempower the worshipping community.

11

Divine Silence Broken in Compassion

For a long time I have held my peace,
I have kept still and restrained myself;
Now I will cry out like a woman in labor,
I will gasp and pant. (Isa 42:14)

THE SILENCE OF GOD is a palpable reality in the life of the world. It cannot be denied. God is often unresponsive to the urgent prayers of desperate people in dire circumstance. We do not know why God is sometimes silent and unresponsive. In his mocking at the silence of Baal in the context at Mt. Carmel Elijah teasingly offers excuses for Baal's failure to answer:

> Surely he is a god; either he is meditating, or he has wandered away, or he is on a journey, or perhaps he is asleep and must be awakened. (1 Kgs 18:27)

Elijah offers four possible explanations for divine silence that are derisive: Baal is meditating, Baal has wandered off, Baal is on a journey, or Baal is sleeping.[1] None of these, however, is a serious proposal that might apply to YHWH's silence. The purpose of the prophet is only to reduce Baal to an object of ridicule.

---

1. Sweeney, *I & II Kings*, 228. A note in the Targum suggests that "wandered off" might mean "gone to relieve himself." This is poetic imagination without textual support.

III. The Riddle of Silence and Speech

I.

The textual tradition of Israel is more serious about YHWH's silence and understands it in terms of covenantal alienation. The book of Lamentations is Israel's powerful reflection on God's silence in that long moment of displacement in the exile. Kathleen O'Connor can speak of "them missing voice" of God in the midst of Israel's needful circumstance in the book of Lamentations:

> God's voice is missing and the book is God-abandoned. But primarily because God is silent, Lamentations expresses human experiences of abandonment with full force. And because God never speaks, the book honors voices of pain. Lamentations is a house of sorrow because there is no speech from God.[2]

When we come to the book of Isaiah in which our text is situated, the moral dimension of God's silence in response to Israel's covenantal infidelity is front and center. At the outset in chapter 1, the Isaiah tradition dismisses the phony piety and worship of Israel, and rejects liturgical approaches that Israel might make to YHWH:

> I cannot endure solemn assemblies with iniquity.
> Your new moons and your appointed festivals
>   my soul hates;
> they have become a burden to me,
>   I am weary of bearing them.
> When you stretch out your hands,
>   I will hide my eyes from you;
> even though you make many prayers,
>   I will not listen;
> your hands are full of blood. (Isa 1:13–15)

The dismissal is a firm resolve from YHWH:

> I cannot endure;
>   I am weary;
>   I will hide my eyes;
>   I will not listen.

These harsh rejections by YHWH give the lie to the easy assumptions of Israel's worship and beyond that to the credulous conviction of being God's chosen people to whom God is unconditionally committed. This harsh

---

2. O'Conner, *Lamentations and the Tears of the World*, 15.

prophetic tone in Isaiah denies, in ancient Israel and among us, that God is always on call and ready to respond to us.

According to the normative narrative it because God "went silence" that Jerusalem was destroyed and Israel was deported. The result of divine silence was not only devastating but was experienced as irreversible. For that reason the book of Lamentations ends, after the doxology of 5:19, the wonderment of 5:20, and the petitions of 5:21, with a thought that God may "utterly reject" and "be angry beyond measure" (v. 22). Thus the wonderment of 5:20 concerns the harsh verbs, "forget, forsake," that is, to give up on covenantal commitments. The long silence of exile invites such an unbearable probe.

The thought that God's silence is an indignant response to covenantal violation and alienation is directly and frontally affirmed in the exilic poetry of Isaiah:

> For a brief moment I abandoned you . . .
> In overflowing wrath for a moment
>   I hid my face from you (Isa 54:7–8).

This harsh acknowledgement is the culmination of the imagery utilized already in Hos 2:2–13. In that poem the prophet appeals to marital imagery in order to delineate the infidelity of Israel toward YHWH. The poets in ancient Israel clearly understood that the depth and seriousness of covenantal infidelity could not be adequately articulated in the symmetrical rhetoric of law and obedience. For that reason the poets must go behind and beyond juridical language to *the rhetoric of relationality*, to the most intimate imagery of marriage (husband-wife) and parenting (parent-child; mother/father//son/daughter). The verbs "forsake, forget" in Lam 5:20 are taken in to refer to marital infidelity; the negatives communicate an end of the covenantal marriage in divorce. The imagery is, perforce, cast in patriarchal terms, but fortunately we have ample literature both to show the problematic of that casting, and to exhibit alternative interpretive options that move suggestively beyond patriarchy.[3]

In Isa 54:7–8 we are given ample ground for God's silence amid exile: the relationship has ended. God has no need or will to speak further to this (legitimately!) rejected partner. The verbs "abandon, hide" bespeak

---

3. See Dempsey, *The Prophets*; O'Brien, *Challenging Prophetic Metaphor*; and Weems, *Battered Love*.

alienation and absence. That stance is said to be "for an instant," but in Israel's life it turns out to be a long "instant" indeed.

That verdict of an abandoned wife is preceded in the poetry by the characterization of a woman disgraced in a patriarchal society. Isaiah 54:4-6 can speak of shame and disgrace, forsakenness and being cut off:

> Do not be discouraged for you will not suffer *disgrace;*
>   for you will forget the *shame* of your youth,
> and the *disgrace* of your widowhood you will remember no more
>   . . .
> For the LORD has called you
>   like a wife *forsaken* and *grieved* in spirit,
> like the wife of a man's youth when she is *cast off.*

These poetic lines speak of rehabilitation, but behind any prospect of rehabilitation is the reality of rejection and its unbearable cost. Indeed such a woman in such a society becomes like a widow forgotten.

And before that, Israel is addressed as a "barren women," a stigma indeed in a patriarchal society (54:1). For without a husband, she cannot bear children. The imagery moves between the *positive of marriage* and *the forlornness of marriage dissolved and motherhood precluded.* In both images the abandoning party (the husband, the would-be father) holds all the power, and can cut off all communication; hence silence!!!

II.

But of course the burden of the exilic poetry of Isaiah (along with other exilic poets in Israel) is to move beyond that alienation and to break the silence.[4] One strategy for getting beyond the alienation is to summon Israel to repent. If the fickle wife or the would-be mother would admit fault, the relationship could be restored and the honor of the husband-father would be vindicated.[5] The poets, however, understood that a summons to repent was no adequate strategy for restoration of the relationship. Calls for repentance had long been sounded to no effect.

Thus the poets must go deeper into the mystery of intimacy. Jeremiah asserts *divine forgiveness* as the ground for a future (Jer 31:34). Ezekiel articulates *divine self-esteem* as the basis for restoration (36:22-32). But the

---

4. Programmatically see Gerhard von Rad, *Old Testament Theology,* vol. 2: *The Theology of Israel's Prophetic Traditions.*

5. See Lapsley, *Can These Bones Live?*

Divine Silence Broken in Compassion

poetry of Isaiah makes its bid in a pivotal text by transposing the dismissive husband-father into a strong caring mother. In Isa 49:14 the poet has "Zion" (perhaps in liturgical reiteration) quote Lam 5:20 with it pathos-filled verbs, "forsake, forget":

> But Zion said, The LORD has forsaken me,
> my Lord has forgotten me.

The two verbs evoke the rhetorical question of 49:15:

> Can a woman forget her nursing child,
> or show no compassion for the child of her womb?

The appropriate answer to the questions is "no." No, the nursing mother cannot forget the nursling, because her breasts are full and she must have relief by nursing. Phyllis Trible has seen so well the word play in the defining term "compassion" and the biological specificity of "womb," for in Hebrew the two terms are the same with different vowel pointing.[6] Thus "compassion" is the tender passionate devotion of a mother to a child, to the child who has emerged wondrously from her womb. The term "compassion" with its continuing force of *womb-like tenderness* is twice used in the assuring response to the negative verdicts of Isa 54:7–8:

> but with great *compassion* I will gather you . . .
> but with everlasting love I will have *compassion* on you.

The obvious answer to the questions of 49:15 is "no." Except that the poet can entertain the possibility that even a nursing mother might forget. We expect the compassionate God to be like a nursing mother. But by the end of v. 15 the compassionate God is *unlike a nursing mother,* because the compassionate God "will never forget you." This affirmation means to answer the questions of Lam 5:20 that is repeated in Isa 49:14 and to insist that even during the "instant" of abandonment in 54:7–8, YHWH, the mother-God with *womb-like compassion* has remembered all through the abandonment. And because YHWH has remembered all through the abandonment, the abandonment and the silence it brings with it, are not and cannot be the final reality. The relation cannot end there!

We may pause to be dazzled by the courageous audacious articulation of the poet who is able to "imagine" YHWH out beyond a bottomless sulking indignation of an offended father or husband. The offended husband

---

6. Trible, *God and the Rhetoric of Sexuality,* 31–59.

becomes the compassionate mother. As result, the barren one can sing with new historical possibility:

> Sing, O barren one who did not bear;
> > burst into song and shout,
> > you who have not been in labor!
> For the children of the desolate woman will be more
> > than the children of her that is married, says the LORD.
> Enlarge the site of your tent,
> > and let the curtains of your habitations be stretched out;
> do not hold back; lengthen your cords
> > and strengthen your stakes.
> For you shall spread out to the right and to the left,
> > and your descendants will possess the nations
> and will settle the desolate towns. (54:1–3)

As a result, the abandoned wife can trust "your husband" (v. 5). As result the silence is broken. The earth (most particularly Jerusalem) is filled with singing, because the abandoning husband has restored the wife, because the barren mother has given birth (see 66:7–11).

Who knew? I hazard that *the indignant father* did not know, for that father cherished his pride too much. I surmise that *the betrayed husband* did not know, because he was preoccupied with his reputation. Neither *God as father* nor *God as husband* knew, because the father-husband-God was trapped in old patterns of pride, indignation, and self-esteem that precluded any new gesture.

So who knew? Well, the poet knew. The poet knew how to break the silence by resituating YHWH in new imagery.[7] The poet understood that there would be no future as long as God continued to reside in images of an offended husband. The poet discerned in an acute way that the future would be frustrated as long as the violated father remained preoccupied with the violation.

In a daring sweep God is in invited (summoned?) to new images that redefine God's capacity toward Israel (and the world) beyond indignation, pride, self-esteem, and cherished reputation. That newness for God was permitted by images of a nursing mother no longer preoccupied with herself, but now completely given over in vulnerability to the requirement

---

7. I speak of the poet as the ones who ran the risks. Since we variously confess that these texts are "inspired," I have no resistance to the thought that these poets were led by the Spirit of God.

of the child.8 [8] For that reason the rhetoric now permits compassion, that deeply felt mystery of womb-like generativity.

III.

It is in this flood of images that our text is situated. The poetic imagery is not logical and it cannot be parsed. It is the overflow of passion that defies all of our explanatory schemes as the poet processes the heart of God. What we get is God's self-disclosure in which God attests the unspoken turmoil of God in the struggle between *self-regard* and *self-giving passion*. In Isa 42:14 we get the two lines of "then" followed by two lines of "now" that reject the silence of "then." In the two lines of "then," the poet has God reflect on times past, "a long time." We are not told how long, but we may judge that it is since the first deportation from Jerusalem. From then until 540 BCE (when the poem is dated) is a long time. It is a long time to "hold peace, keep still, restrain" self. It turns out, in this verse, that that long season of divine silence was not a time of absence or indifference. It was a time when God wanted to intervene and did not. We are not told why God was so long silent, only that the silence was a freighted silence of a God who never ceased to care or to notice. There is no suggestion of divine indifference; nor is the any hint that the silence is designed to teach Israel a lesson. If, as I have suggested, it required a poet to parse the imagery in fresh ways, perhaps the silence was so long until the right poet showed up to give proper voice.

Henry Sloan Coffin probes the life of God in these two lines and suggests the sleepless, restless life of God, not unlike a parent who suffers and waits in silence for a recalcitrant child to "come to himself" (see Luke 15:17).[9] Such long waiting is, says Coffin, the "eternal insomnia" of God, endless sleepless nights of travail, quite in contrast to the "impenetrable tranquility" of the gods of indifference.

---

8. In "A Brief Statement of "Faith," 38, the Presbyterian confession nicely joins allusions to *the nursing mother* (Isa 49:14–15) and *the welcoming father* (Luke 15:20), both of whom maximized conventional social roles for the sake of the relationship:

> Like a mother who will not forsake her nursing child,
> like a father who runs to welcome the prodigal home,
> God is faithful still.

9. Coffin, "The Book of Isaiah, Exposition," 473.

III. The Riddle of Silence and Speech

The turn in the third line of v. 14 is decisive. *Now* is unlike that long time past. For that long time, YHWH could resist speaking or acting. But *now, now* the energy and force is like a woman in labor. The daring imagery we have reviewed thus far is now pushed even further, imagining biological processes in which the mother God brings new futures for Israel. As we had three verbs of restraint in the season of "then," so now we get three verbs of urgent generativity: cry out, gasp, pant." The move to *now* is not accomplished because of any change in Israel. Nor is it accomplished by any changed disposition on God's part. All that is required for *now* is that the time is right. This is indeed "the fullness of time" when, according to the imagery, the pregnancy has run its course. Like every such birth, the child (that is, Israel's future) is the outcome of a mother who does all the work. The mother God could not wait longer. The silence is broken. The future begins. The past is over. Like every new birth, it is a time for joy.

The poet does not linger with the birth imagery very long. In vv. 15–16, we get a series of first-person declarations, but now the scope of divine engagement is not the intimacy of birth or family. Now the God who is activated is preoccupied with creation, cosmic upheaval, and safe passage home. The poetry is reminiscent of the water in the desert:

> Then the eyes of the blind shall be opened,
>   and the ears of the deaf unstopped;
> then the lame shall leap like a deer,
>   and the tongue of the speechless sing for joy.
> For waters shall break forth in the wilderness,
>   and streams in the desert.
> The burning sand shall become a pool,
>   and the thirsty ground springs of water. (35:5–7)

That scene, moreover, issues in safe passage home with the nullification of all "sorrow and sadness" (35:8–10).

The recital of divine resolve in our passage culminates with the assurance of v. 16: "I will not forsake them." The poet returns to the specificity of birth in 45:10 for a different reason. In 45:1, the poet declares that God well send a *goi* messiah to Israel, Cyrus the Persian. Such a prospect evoked hostility and now God responds to the resistance to God's intent:

> Woe to anyone who says to a father, "What are you begetting?"
>   or to a woman, "With what are you in labor?" (45:10)

The imagery concerns both *the sexual activity of the father* and *the labor of the mother*. In neither case will the biology of newness be questioned. So, says the poet, God's promise for wellbeing via a *goi* will not be questioned.

IV.

The silence is broken and the world begins anew! The silence is broken by God's readiness to be cast in a wholly new role . . . because old roles of juridical requirement permit no newness. The silence is broken because the old imagining kept all parties boxed in alienation. But birth time requires and evokes new imagination. At birth time we find new names and new patterns of relationship. We may reflect on how it is that we (and God!) are kept in thrall to old functions, old images, old patterns of alienation, and old certitudes all of which end in despair.

Paul takes up the imagery of Isaiah for the new world of the gospel:

> For the creation waits with eager longing for the revealing of the children of God; for the creation was subjected to futility, not of its own will but by the will of the one who subjected it, in hope that the creation itself will be set free from its bondage to decay and will obtain the freedom of the glory of the children of God. We know that the whole creation has been groaning in *labor pains* until now; and not only the creation, but we ourselves, who have the first fruits of the Spirit, groan inwardly while we wait for adoption, the redemption of our bodies. (Rom 8:19–23)

Paul goes cosmic with the imagery of birth; but Isaiah had already seen that the imagery cannot be contained within the life of Israel.

The later years of the twentieth century and now the twenty-first century, under the aegis of many forms of a liberation hermeneutic, witness many different populations and peoples coming to consciousness about futures given in an emancipatory justice. It is as though for many peoples we have, in God's providence, arrived at the fullness of time. We are watching as new worlds of justice are being birthed.

The "long time" of God's silence, however, still operates in many vexed venues. Such venues include many practices of injustice, but the defining "long time" in our society is that of slavery and its current toxic residue in White Rage.[10] We are permitted by this text to recognize that the "long time" of bondage is not marked by divine indifference, absence, or disregard. We

---

10. Anderson, *White Rage*.

are, moreover, given reason to trust that the "long time" of bondage is not forever. The text attests the fullness of time that is in God's hands. We may expect that the end of the "long time" will yet again be the work of poets. The artistic enterprise has as its work imagining otherwise. Such artistry, we may conclude, may impinge even upon God. Reimagining is human work; but it is the gift of the Spirit who attests that the long time of silence is not forever. Full time comes when

> The blind receive their sight, the lame walk, the lepers are cleansed, the deaf hear, the dead are raised, the poor have good news brought to them (Luke 7:22).

As that happens, there is no more silence, on earth or in heaven.

12

Speaking Hebrew amid the Empire

When he had given him permission, Paul stood on the steps and motioned for to the people for silence; and when there was a great hush, he addressed them in the Hebrew language... (Acts 21:40)

IN THE BOOK OF Acts Paul lives in a triangle amid *officials of the Roman Empire* who extend to him judicial even if suspicious protection, and *Jews* who reject and his message with hostility. In our narrative (Acts 21:27—22:29) "the Jews" (a stereotypical usage in the narrative) incite "the crowd" against Paul. We get at the outset a scene in which "the crowd shouted" (21:34), the mob became violent (21:35), and the crowd "kept shouting" (21:36). At the end of the narrative, "they shouted" (22:22). In both the introductory episode (21:36) and the concluding episode (22:22), the crowd shouted "away with him," adding in 22:22, "He should not be allowed to live." This is, in the horizon of Luke, the same crowd that shouted against Jesus, "Crucify, crucify him" (Luke 23:21). As Luke styles it, the Jewish crowd wanted for Paul the same execution it had wanted for Jesus.

Paul is removed from the "lynching crowd" by the Roman tribune who arrests him at the behest of the crowd (21:33); but by the end of the narrative Paul is identified as a Roman citizen, a fact that may have unnerved the tribune because he has arrested a Roman citizen (22:29). Indeed, it turns out in 22:28 that the tribune himself had purchased his Roman citizenship, whereas Paul was born a citizen, thus giving him the upper hand. By the end of the narrative, the crowd has been overruled by the imperial officer, and the imperial officer in turn has come to a new respect for Paul's status as a citizen. Thus Paul emerges from the narrative both validated in the eyes of the empire, and protected from his adversaries. By the end of the narrative, the crowd fades away before imperial authority.

That narrative at the beginning (21:27–36) and the end (22:22–29), however, is simply framing for the witness of Paul offered in the long speech at the center of our text. His testimony is introduced by an exchange with the Roman tribune in 21:37–40. In that terse exchange

—Paul asks to speak before the tribune on his own behalf;

—the tribune queries Paul about his capacity to speak Greek, because the tribune wonders if Paul is a certain trouble-making Egyptian.

—Paul answers, "I am a Jew" and is thereby rightly identified, and is not that Egyptian.

His proper identification gains for Paul from the tribune permission to speak; it is this freedom to speak that is the whole point of Paul's effort with the tribune. He receives permission so that in Luke's telling the Roman tribune gives Paul freedom to address the people, that is, the Jewish crowd that had cried out against him.

I.

Our attention to this passage turns on two interpretive points. First, the narrative confirms that Paul is bilingual; he can speak Greek to the imperial officer and Hebrew (Aramaic) to the assembled crowd. In a study of speech and silence (in which we are engaged), the matter of being bilingual is of immense importance, because it allows Paul (and the church that he embodies and represents) to traverse two very different worlds. In the narrative of the book of Acts, Luke has a definitive interest in the bilingual reality that permits the early church to flourish in the Roman Empire. Paul's capacity for bilingual communication is perhaps to be understood in the wake of two narrative reports in the Old Testament in which being bilingual matters.

First, in 2 Kgs 18:17–36 the Assyrian ambassador to Jerusalem confronts King Hezekiah at the wall in the city. The burden of the ambassador

Speaking Hebrew amid the Empire

is to issue a threatening ultimatum to the King Hezekiah, supported by the presence and power of the Assyrian army. In response to the intimidating speech of the ambassador, the mediator for Hezekiah asks the Assyrian ambassador:

> Please speak to your servant in the Aramaic language; for we understand it; do not speak to us in the language of Judah within the hearing of the people who are on the wall. (2 Kgs 18:26)

The king wants the ambassador to utilize international language (Aramaic) because the common folk of Jerusalem could not understand and would not be frightened. Hezekiah wants the ominous military reality to be concealed from his people by using a language not popularly known. The Assyrian ambassador, however, refuses:

> But the Rabshakeh said to them, "Has my master sent me to speak these words to your master and to you, and not to the people sitting on the wall, who are doomed with you to eat their own dung and to drink their own urine?" Then the Rabshakeh stood and called out in a loud voice in the language of Judah . . . (2 Kgs 18:27-28)

The "language of Judah" is Hebrew. The imperial official refused the finesse of international language and used Hebrew because he wanted the subjects of Hezekiah to be properly terrified in order to deflate resistance to the Assyrian army. As the narrative eventuates, the king is himself greatly terrified and is finally rescued only by the inexplicable intervention of the prophet Isaiah (2 Kgs 19:6-7, 21-28) that results in the inexplicable deliverance of the city (vv. 35-37). It turns out that Hebrew, the language of faith, functioned as the tongue of fear and intimidation. The Assyrian ambassador was fully bilingual and knew which language to speak when.

In a second text the same tricky capacity to be bilingual is evident in the narrative of Daniel as the wise, patient Jew who skillfully negotiates between the requirements of the Babylonian Empire and the specific narrative of Jewish identity. This trickiness is made explicit:

> Among them [civil servant recruits in the empire] were Daniel, Hananiah, Mishael, and Azariah, from the tribe of Judah. The palace master gave them other names: Daniel he called Belteshazzar, Hananiah he called Shadrach, Mishael he called Meshach, and Azariah he called Abednego. (Dan 1:6-7)

King Nebuchadnezzar had recruited "some of the Israelites" for imperial civil service:

III. The Riddle of Silence and Speech

> Then the king commanded his palace master Ashpenaz to bring some of the Israelites of the royal family and of the nobility, young men without physical defect and handsome, versed in every branch of wisdom, endowed with knowledge and insight, and competent to serve in the king's palace; they were to be taught the literature and language of the Chaldeans. (Dan 1:3-4)

Because they were to serve the empire, they are "to be taught the language of the Chaldeans," that is Akkadian (1:4). As a result we are given the Jewish names of Daniel and his three friends. But then we are told the "other names" assigned by the palace master. It is ironic that we popularly know Daniel by his Jewish name, but his three friends we know only by their imperial names: Shadrach, Meshach, and Abednego. Their Jewish identity has among us long since been forgotten.

The matter of *Jewish identity* and *Babylonian service* (obedience!) is a core issue of the book of Daniel, so that the interplay of Hebrew and Aramaic in the book of Daniel is not simply an accident of transmission and translation, but is a deliberate strategy to exhibit the requirements of a bilingual faith.[1] Thus in what follows Daniel will faithfully bear witness to the God of Israel, but without the rhetoric of Jewish specificity. As a result, even Nebuchadnezzar, the head of an alien empire, is won over to affirm the God of Israel:

> The king said to Daniel: "Truly your God is God of gods and Lord of kings, and a revealer of mysteries, for you have been able to reveal this mystery." (2:47)

> Therefore I make a decree: Any people, nation, or language that utters blasphemy against the God of Shadrach, Meshach, and Abednego shall be torn limb from limb, and their houses laid in ruins; for there is no other god who is able to deliver in this way. (3:29)

> Now I, Nebuchadnezzar, praise and extol and honor the King of heaven,
> for all his works are truth,
> and his ways are justice;
> and he is able to bring low those who walk in pride. (4:37)

In chapter 6, moreover, Nebuchadnezzar is echoed by Darius, the Persian:

> For he is the living God,

---

1. See Portier-Young, "Languages of Identity and Obligation."

> enduring forever.
> His kingdom shall never be destroyed,
> and his dominion has no end.
> He delivers and rescues,
> he works signs and wonders in heaven and on earth;
> for he has saved Daniel
> from the power of the lion. (6:26–27)

In the text concerning Hezekiah, the imperial ambassador agilely employs bilingual skills as an affront to the king. But in the book of Daniel, the wise Jew, Daniel, manages by bilingual finesse to create doxological space for the God of Israel. The capstone of Daniel's success, I suggest, is in the wise counsel he gives to Nebuchadnezzar about royal conduct and policy in the face of divine judgment:

> Atone for your sins with righteousness, and your iniquities with mercy to the oppressed, so that your posterity may be prolonged. (4:27)

Clearly Daniel gives the Babylonian king (unasked) Jewish counsel, so that Torah measures are operative in the empire, Torah norms are acknowledged by Nebuchadnezzar in 4:27 as "truth and justice."

I have taken this long with these Old Testament texts because I suggest the linguistic maneuver by Paul in our narrative text concerning Greek and Hebrew reflects the same tricky matrix that requires bilingual finesse. In a quick paragraph Paul moves from *Greek* spoken with the imperial tribune to *Hebrew* in which he addresses the Jewish crowd. He speaks his mother-tongue that is also a language outside the purview of imperial grammarians. Thus our first accent concerns the linguistic dexterity of Paul's testimony.

II.

Our second primary accent is the remarkable interaction Paul had with the crowd when he began to speak in Hebrew. He had identified himself to the tribune as a Jew (Acts 21:39), and he demonstrated to the tribune that identity by the Hebrew that follows. He asked for silence from the crowd; and there was "a great hush."[2] This is stunning moment in the narrative. Only a few verses before this the same crowd had shouted "away with him"

---

2. The term "hush" is used in the New Testament only here and in Rev 8:1, a text that will be the subject of our final study.

III. The Riddle of Silence and Speech

(21:36). But now there is silence. This is not imposed or coerced silence. This is anticipatory silence. Presumably the crowd was not privy to the exchange Paul had just had with the tribune. The crowd must have wondered how Paul was permitted to speak after he had been arrested. They waited in silence. H addressed them in Hebrew," that is in Aramaic (21:40). The narrative reports: "When they heard him addressing them in Hebrew, they became even more quiet" (22:2). More quiet! More quiet because the Jews were drawn to their mother tongue. Perhaps these Jews in Jerusalem were weary of too much imperial talk issued in imperial language, so that their own city was rendered in a way foreign to them. Perhaps because Paul had parleyed with the imperial tribune they expected more imperial talk from him. But he spoke and surprised them. He spoke Hebrew! And he said, "I am a Jew" (22:3). That surely was reassuring to this Jewish crowd, because they had accused him of teaching against our people, our law, and this place (21:28).

For an instant they must have withdrawn their charge that they had just uttered against him. They accused him of bringing a Greeks into the temple and thereby defiling the holy place. But now he said to them, "I am a Jew." More than that, Paul states his credentials (22:3). More than that he assures these Jews that he had been a vigorous adversary to "this way," the radical way of Christ (v. 4). This was a welcome assurance! He not only spoke their language. He shared their hostility to the new movement and their resistance to "this way" that seemed to them to violate Jewish norms.

So far, so good! The "hush" must have prevailed for that much of Paul's defense. But then his defense takes an unexpected turn, even if spoken in the right language. After 22:6 he reiterates his story of his inexplicable encounter, the bright light, the direct address from "Jesus of Nazareth," his becoming blind, the aid of Ananias, his regaining of his sight, his baptism by Ananias, and his witness to the death of Stephen. And the finally this: "He said to me: Go, for I will send you far away to the Gentiles" (22:21). The entire narrative ends in a commission directly from Jesus. He is sent to the Gentiles. If we consider the entire speech from 22:3-21 we note the curious envelop. It begins, "I am a Jew." It ends, "Go to the Gentiles." The narrative reports, already in 21:21, that he is accused of violating the most precious norms of his people.

The crowd must have been, to say the least, bewildered by his words. His familiar speech in familiar cadence ended with the shockingly unfamiliar. The narrative has it: "Up to this point they listened to him, but then they shouted" (22:22). Up to this point! There must have been a pause while his testimony sank in. And then "the hush" ended. The crowd had grown "quieter," but now could be quiet no more. The shout resumed from 21:36 (22:22).

In our study of silence I am fascinated by this moment of hush that could not be sustained very long. The hush was because of Hebrew speech. The hush provided the crowd a chance to consider that perhaps they had misread Paul, and that he really was "one of us." Indeed in his credentials and in his speech he asserts that he is "one of us" (22:3).

III.

This text witnesses to a great silence that is dramatically broken:

—The silence is broken in vigorous hostility by Paul's Jewish audience when they finally understand what Paul is saying about Gentiles (22:22–23). His fellow Jews broke the silence because they understood that Paul's new life violated the body of old norms, a violation that was indeed unacceptable to them.

—But the crowd broke the silence because Paul, in his testimony, had broken the silence. He himself had heretofore settled into the silence of conventional faith "according to our ancestral law." But then he narrates a radical turn in his life in which it became impossible to continue with the old exclusionary norms.

—But Paul broke the silence because he himself found the silence of his conventional life being broken by none other than Jesus of Nazareth. Thus: I answered, "Who are you, Lord?" Then he said to me, "I am Jesus of Nazareth whom you are persecuting (22:8).

I fell into a trance and saw Jesus saying to me, '"Hurry and get out of Jerusalem quickly, because they will not accept your testimony about me . . . Then he said to me, "Go, for I will send you far away to the Gentiles (22:1–21).

Jesus broke the silence and interrupted Paul's zealous mission of persecution. Jesus broke the silence of Paul's conventional faith. Jesus broke the silence by dispatching Paul to a new mandate that violated all his long held passion and discernment. There could be nothing more radical than "Gentiles" (22:21). It is his notice of the Gentiles that broke the silence!

III. The Riddle of Silence and Speech

These three silence-breakings, by *the crowd*, by *Paul*, and by *Jesus of Nazareth*, constitute a radical reset of faith in which Paul—and the entire movement that the led—featured nothing less than embrace of the Other. The move out of any tribal arrangement to God's large goodness is the decisive silence-breaker of all time. And the rest, as we say, is history. That silence-breaking had an immense impact on the character and intent of the early church. Paul is credited with the "mission to the Gentiles." But alongside Paul is the evangelical breaking of silence for and by Peter. His narrative in Acts 10 is as decisive and inexplicable as that of Paul in Acts 9. It is to the same point: "God shows no partiality!" (Acts 10:34). Peter may not call unclean what God has declared to be clean (Acts 10:15–16). And no less for John (the other theologian of the apostolic church) is the silence broken: "Other sheep I have not of this fold" (John 10:16).

The great silence that we regularly try to sustain is the silence of excluding the other, of not noticing the other, not hearing, not taking seriously, not acknowledging. It is the temptation of every community, and certainly of every community that imagines it possesses the truth, to want to fence out all the others. So it is with white racism. So it is with American exceptionalism. So it is with "The one holy catholic, apostolic Church" in its various modalities. So it is in our pride and in our fear. So it habitually is with us as it was with the shouting crowd that broke the hush. But in the middle of the shouting crowd that wanted to expel Paul is Jesus of Nazareth who was not silenced.

The news for Paul, however, is that the silence of exclusion has been broken. The other is before us as brother, sister, and neighbor. We have seen in Mark 7:28 that the legitimacy of the other ("dogs" after "children") was a shock to Jesus. We have seen that the legitimacy of the other (now declared clean!) was a shock to Peter and to Paul. And now we see it as a shock to this crowd. The crowd thought that by its aggressive hostility that it could continue its tradition of exclusion. The crowd wanted "away with him!" (Acts 21:36).

In the apostolic witness, however, the "other" is here to stay. From this Paul will spend his life bearing witness to the legitimacy of the other in the sphere of God's goodness and grace. In his epistles, he witnesses to God's grace that overrides all exclusions of Jew/Greek, slave/free, male/female (Gal 3:28). That silence-breaking reality is always again rediscovered in this silence-breaking tradition, variously by Augustine, by Luther, by Barth, by Oscar Romero, by an endless succession of liberationists, even perhaps by us amid our xenophobic propensity. Paul's breaking of the silenced was in Hebrew in a move beyond imperial Greek. Hebrew is perhaps the primary silence-breaking dialect because its form is recurringly elusive and endlessly open to interpretation in ways that refuse absolutizing closure. But of course the silence-breaking persists in many languages, among many tongues and nations. It turns out that no single language has a monopoly on silence-breaking. The imperial tribune wondered whether Paul spoke Greek. He did! And since that moment the apostolic testimony out toward the Gentiles is sounded in many languages. That testimony arises in the midst of a great "hush," and then comes a torrent of doxology.

13

Voiced Pain Unanswered

Every day I call to you, O LORD;
    I spread out my hands to you. (Ps 88:9)

ISRAEL'S PSALMS OF LAMENT, complaint, and protest characteristically end in confidence, hope, and praise to God. It is as though through the dramatic process of the Psalm (in utterance or in performance) the speaker has received signals of assurance from God that God is attentive and will act in transformative ways toward the speaker. We do not know whether such a signal comes through the *liturgical process* (as has often been proposed) or whether it comes through a *psychological turn* by the speaker. In any case, these psalms regularly move in an affirmative direction and end in a conviction of wellbeing assured by a responding God who hears and answers.

I.

This oft-reiterated confidence in God lies behind the conviction of the church that God does indeed reliably answer prayer. Thus the prophet can have God say:

> Before they call I will answer,
>   while they are yet speaking I will hear. (Isa 65:24)

That is, God is so eager to answer that God does not even wait until we finish speaking before God answers back. And in the later tradition of the church we pray in the form of a collect with immense confidence:

> Almighty and everlasting God, you are always more ready to hear than we are to pray, and to give more than we either desire or deserve.[1]

This artistic formulation suggests that the hard part of prayer is our willingness to pray, thus another example of the silencing that is so common among us, a reluctance to tell the truth of our lives before God. According to the collect, speaking such honest prayer is the hard part; the other part of prayer, God's response is assured, indeed is "always," "always more ready" (than we are ready), thus the hard part is on our end of the conversation. On God's end there is no hard part because of who God is.

But of course such confident trust in God's ready responsiveness—in the tradition of the Psalms and in the assertion of the church—does not fully square with the lived experience of the faithful. Of course we know the convenient cliché that protects God: "God always answers prayer but sometimes the answer is no." Such an explanatory offer, however, is more clever than it is helpful. For anyone in anguish it is no more than religious kitsch. The reality of lived experience is that sometimes (thus violating a comfortable, confident "always") there is no answer. Many honest people of faith are wont to reverse the prayer, "We are always more ready to pray than God is to hear." The "always" of the assurance, I suggest, misstates the dialogical freedom of God, though of course I know that is in high assured theology *God's freedom* is always in the service of *God's unfailing faithfulness* toward us.

II.

In the face of such confidence as expressed in the tradition, we may be glad for the dissenting opinion of Psalm 88.[2] This notorious Psalm violates the easier consensus of the tradition and of church conviction. It is, to be sure, only a wee dissent and not a programmatic proposal as with the consensus. But the fact that the psalm came to be included in the inventory of the

---

1. "Proper 22," in *The Book of Common Prayer*, 234.
2. The most helpful, thoughtful commentary on Ps 88 is by Janowski, *Arguing with God*, 218–47; see also Lindstrom, *Suffering and Sin*, 196–217.

III. The Riddle of Silence and Speech

Psalms is important, because it suggests that the tradition is honest enough to voice and take seriously an alternative judgment that is surely grounded in lived experience.

The Psalm is organized around three insistent assertions, each of which serves to intensify the urgent dissent. In v. 1 the first word is the Israelite name of God identified in an intimate and personal way with as God "of my salvation."[3] This address might serve to give God an alert to be attentive "at night," perhaps this night when I cry to you. Such cries do arise at night when one experiences alone the force of the unformed, unmanaged chaos of darkness. The verb "cry" is used twice. The psalmist knows, even before night comes, that there will arise the cry of desperate petition that seeks to mobilize God, if God will only listen. Likely the psalmist has this anticipation for the coming night because she can remember previous cries in the night. The speaker seeks and must have this ally in the night, because the speaker cannot cope alone with such chaotic reality. The speaker can expect that God will "incline your ear" so that all may be well. But the speaker also has good reason to think that God may not respond, perhaps a negative expectation grounded in past experience. Thus the opening appeal is uttered in ambivalence, hoping but perhaps frustrated at the outset.

The second like statement is a slight advance (v. 9). In v. 1 the statement concerns a coming night. But now, it is "every day," as though the prayer had gone on a long time. The second statement again names YHWH in a vocative, thus summoning to attention. The opening line is reinforced by a second, parallel line, so that the word is accompanied by a gesture of need, vulnerability, and submissiveness.

The third such cry, again with a vocative and the divine name, now concerns a cry (prayer) "in the morning," as though the long night had been unrelieved (v. 13). Thus the three statements concern in sequence, "at night, every day, in the morning," that is, all the time! We are not told why the petition is so urgent, incessant, and insistent. Indeed it is the marvel of such poetry to be so specific in its intensity, and yet to leave matters completely open so that we, as belated readers and speakers, may fill in the Psalm and its cry with our own particular urgencies.

There is, in the face of these three urgent insistences, no divine answer: not at night, not all day long, not in the morning! It does no good to proclaim that "It is morning in America" nor does it ring true to assert

---

3. See Gerstenberger, *Theologies of the Old Testament*, 25–110 and *passim*; and Albertz and Schmitt, *Family and Household Religion in Ancient Israel and the Levant*.

"It is morning in ancient Israel," when the silence of the night remains unbroken into the day. This is the truth of this Psalm that readily violates the normative genre and that willingly contradicts the settled conviction of the church. God does not answer! The speaker in this Psalm is not unlike the character of Job who, in the face of the admonition of his friends, refuses to scrap the truth of his own experience for the sake of maintaining the consensus. This Psalm readily becomes a resource for many people who have just such an experience. Our theme is silence, but the silence here is not human reticence. The speaker readily breaks the silence, readily refuses awed restraint or docile deference. Indeed the work and energy of the psalm is exactly a refusal of silence before God. Well, yes, there is silence. It is God's silence, for God, inside this psalm, refuses to be summoned or mobilized, even by urgently voiced need.[4]

This leaves the psalmist with what must have been an exceedingly difficult position. What to do in the face of God's unimaginable, inexplicable silence? Clearly it did not occur to the psalmist to desist from speaking. She has already refused such silence in our previous studies:

—She has refused the pious silence of the priests (see Habakkuk);

—She has refused the coercive silence of the powerful (see Pharaoh and Amaziah);

—She has rejected the self-imposed silence of shame or fear (see Ps 32).

She has refused silence because she is confident of the legitimacy of her own speech. I submit that she has come to understand herself as a fully entitled member of a dialogic covenant who is authorized by that membership to speak and to insist on divine response. To fall back into deferential silence in response to divine silence would be to renege on this membership and she would thereby forfeit his identity. She however entertains no thought of such a renege and no prospect for such a forfeiture. She will speak out of her treasured membership at night, every day, in the morning!

> 4. This is the silence of which Shusaku Endo, *Silence*, 153, 173, 266, writes:
>
> > Lord, why are you silent? Why are you always silent . . . ? . . . The Lord will not abandon you forever. He it is who washes our wounds; his is the hand that wipe away our blood. The Lord will not be silent forever . . . Lord, it is now that you should break the silence. You must not remain silent. Prove that you are justice, that you are goodness, that you are love. You must say something to show the world that you are the august one.

III.

But that decision leaves open for the psalmist (as for those who replicate the psalmist) what to say and how to pray when there is no answer. I submit that the relentless speech of the psalmist addressed to God is an anticipation of Jesus' parable through which he instructs his disciples on how to pray (Luke 18:1–7). The lead-in character in the parable is a widow, thus without a male advocate in a patriarchal society. She suffers injustice and wants the redress of justice. The psalmist is like that before God. Like the widow she has no standing ground. But she must be heard, because he speaks out of wants redress, that is, "salvation" (v. 1).

The one whom the widow addresses in the story is a judge with life-or-death authority who "neither feared God nor had respect for people" (v. 2). The parable daringly suggests a God who has no respect for people and fears nothing, not even God's own reputation. Thus if we may transport the parable back into the Psalm, the psalmist is not unlike a relentless widow, and the God whom she addresses is like a judge who cares for nobody. What a transaction! Nothing pious here. Nothing deferential. Nothing assured or assumed. But, says Jesus to his disciples, "Pray like this." The parable is so offensive because it recasts prayer away from conventional comfortable piety to life-or-death urgency with little chance of success. It is, moreover, compelling for the same reason that it is offensive. The psalmist is as persistent in prayer as is the widow.

But of course the petition to the judge succeeds. The unjust, indifferent judge is worn down by the resolve of the widow, and because of the intrinsic legitimacy of justice before which even an unjust judge must yield. Jesus says to his followers, "Pray like that." And keep doing it! Thus I submit that the psalmist prays like the woman in the parable, in the interest of justice that he has not yet received. Such relentless insistence will wear out the judge who will yield in exasperation. And says Jesus, "If you pray that like that you will never lose heart." Thus we may imagine that the three cries of vv. 1–2, 9, and 13 in our Psalm is exactly such persistence as that is commended by Jesus.

IV.

I suggest that the rest of the Psalm, clustered around the three urgent petitions *at night*, *all day long*, and *in the morning*, exhibits a practice of faith that has not lost heart. Almost but not yet lost heart, not yet reduced to silence, not yet giving up in either deference or exasperation. Thus in the face of prayer unanswered, the psalmist prays again, because the God on the other end of the transaction cannot finally evade the intrinsic claims of justice.

We can, I propose, identify three kinds of continuing speech in this Psalm that are sandwiched between the crises of night, all day, and morning. First, this speaker of unanswered cry tried to move God to respond by *providing specific detail to God concerning the dire circumstance of need*. The bid is based on the assumption that if the situation of the speaker (Israel) is drastic enough, God can be moved to compassion. This appeal is based, characteristically in Israel's psalms of lament, on the dramatic (not to say ontological) assumption that God will not know of this dire circumstance unless it is voiced.[5] That is, God, like the psalmist, is a speech-character who depends upon speech.

Thus the psalmist describes a circumstance of death and utilizes three "likenesses" to underscore the point. It is to be remembered that "death" in such rhetoric denotes any form of diminished life, so that the rhetoric of extremity can serve in many circumstances:

> For my soul is full of troubles,
>   and my life draws near to Sheol.
> I am counted among those who go down to the Pit;
>   I am like those who have no help (Ps 88:3–4).

The verbal cluster of "trouble, Sheol, Pit, no help" both portrays utter helplessness and complete need for God's attention. All that stands between the speaker and "non-being" is the attentiveness of God. The appeal to "likeness" intensifies the urgency:

—like the forsaken among the dead;

—like the slain in the grave;

—like those not remembered and cut off (v. 5).

The speaker is not one of those, but she is "like" them and she prays as one of them. God is the last resort of appeal. The description of dire need is continued in v. 15:

---

5. This aspect of lament that recurs in the genre, as in Psalm 88, makes no sense if one assumes the omniscience of God. It is because God does not yet know that the speaker must provide the data; on the point see Fretheim, *The Suffering of God*, chap. 4.

III. The Riddle of Silence and Speech

> Wretched and close to death from my youth up,
> I suffer your terrors; I am desperate.

God is given more specifics of urgent need: "death, terrors, desperate." It is for good reason that Janowski reads the rhetoric in the drama of death. None of that appeal, however, evokes divine response.

Second, the appeal is intensified by *providing additional motivation* for God's engagement by a series of six rhetorical questions:

> Do you work wonders for the dead?
>   Do the shades rise up to praise you?
> Is your steadfast love declared in the grave,
>   or your faithfulness in Abaddon?
> Are your wonders known in the darkness,
>   or your saving help in the land of forgetfulness? (vv. 10–12)

In every case the answer is "no":

No, there are no divine wonders for the dead;

  No, the shades (the dead) do not praise YHWH;

    No, YHWH's *hesed* is not asserted in death;

      No, nor is YHWH"s faithfulness;

        No, YHWH's wonders are not known in darkness.

          No, YHWH's saving help is not remembered there.

That is, in the zone of death (the dead, shades, grave, Abaddon, darkness, forgetfulness) YHWH gets no play. The six questions assume that YHWH wants (needs?) praise. God wants (needs?) to have miracles remembered. God wants (needs?) to have divine faithfulness celebrated. None of that, however, will happen in the zone of death. Thus if God wants (needs?) such affirmation, God had best rescue the speaker who is a reliable singer of praise to YHWH and a trustworthy witness to divine miracles. That is, the response of God and the rescue of the psalmist are not only matters of acute interest to the psalmist; they are (or should be) likewise matters of intense interest to YHWH as well. For that reason YHWH should care enough about YHWH's reputation to act. This is, of course, an act of bribery or flattery; but it does not to work; not even such a calculating choreographed maneuver works! Even that, with such reiterative force, does not move God to act!

Third, the speaker of the Psalm makes a final effort at summoning God to response by *accusations against God that assert God's guilt or that seek to shame God*. Thus we get series of "you" statements that constitute an unqualified assault on God' honor and concerning God's claim to faithfulness. It is clear that the speaker accepts no fault for the failure of their relationship, but holds God fully and singularly accountable:

> *You* have put me in the depths of the Pit,
>   in the regions of dark and deep.
> *Your* wrath lies heavy upon me,
>   and *you* overwhelm me with all your waves.
> *You* have caused my companions to shun me;
>   *you* have made me a thing of horror to them . . .
> *Your* wrath has swept over me;
>   *your* dread assaults destroy me . . .
> *You* have caused friend and neighbor to shun me;
>   companions are in darkness. (vv. 6–8a, 16, 18)

The psalmist does not (or cannot?) identify any of her own failings that would result in such treatment. It is God who has failed![6]

We do not know if this third rhetorical strategy was a last desperate attempt to call God back to covenant, or if is an admission of defeat and helplessness in which the speaker no longer expects anything from God. If the latter is the case, it is even more remarkable that in such defeat the speaker continues the declaration before God. It seems most likely, however, that this is rather an appeal to God's honor, an attempt to recall God to God's own covenantal commitments. Once the speaker has broken the silence, there will be no retreat back into silence. The silence of God is totally inexplicable to the speaker. That divine silence, however, will not silence the psalmist into resignation. Thus even this final desperate rhetorical entry continues to be an act of hope. It is an undefeated insistence that there is none other to address, that there is only this one from whom we may expect listening engagement.

This Job-like act of defiance receives no answer. In Job's final self-defense in 31:35–37, Job still hopes for a response, a hearing. And indeed, Job eventually receives answer in Job 38–41, albeit not an answer he anticipated,

---

6. Lindström, *Suffering and Sin*, 202, 211, is clear that the troubles of the psalmist are not the result of the personal guilt of the speaker: "This Psalm presents, stronger than any other in the individual complaint psalms, the irrationality of YHWH"s dealings with the petitioner . . . [The Psalm] emphasizes the incomprehensible of and unjustified in [sic] the divine action towards the petitioner."

III. The Riddle of Silence and Speech

but nonetheless an answer. By that much he is better off than the psalmist. The psalmist knows that real faith requires dialogic engagement in which both parties must refuse silence. At least the psalmist honors her part of the transaction. Such one-way communication is of course not satisfactory. It is better, however, than silence on the part of both parties, for it allows for the open-ended chance that there will belatedly be answer. Within the scope of this psalm, the speaker has no alternative except to continue to speak and perhaps to continue to escalate and intensify her rhetoric. After all, the one who speaks has not only risked breaking the silence. The speaker is fully aware that she is entitled to such speech before God. We are given no sign here that the speaker is about to forego that bold entitlement.[7]

---

7. Styron, *Sophie's Choice*, 614–15, utilizes this psalm as a "prescription for my torment" of the lead character, Stingo. Styron has the nameless women on the bus commend Psalm 88 as "one fine Psalm" because it allows voiced pain to God in an unbearable situation where there is no response. Stingo cannot believe that he is entitled to such bold voice.

14

Ultimate Awe before the Lamb

When the Lamb opened the seventh seal, there was silence in heaven for about half an hour. (Rev 8:1)

AT THE CENTER OF the book of Revelation is the "revelation" of the seven sealed scrolls that are opened for the church under persecution. The sealed scrolls contain a declaration of the future of the world that has already been determined by the Lord of history, the creator of all that is, who will not countenance wholesale systemic disobedience. The immediate target of the "revelation" is the Roman Empire that was organized as a socio-political theological alternative to the rule of God. But as living testimony the "revelation" of the book of Revelation pertains to every wholesale, systemic defiance of God, surely including the belated defiance of our own circumstance.

I.

The account of the seven sealed scrolls is expressed in freighted, outrageous symbolic rhetoric, because the reality of the world is disobedience that cannot be contained in the conventional logic of the Roman Empire (Rev 6:1—9:21). Thus this *radically alternative vision* of the future of the world under divine judgment requires *radically alternative rhetoric*. It is rhetoric that is regularly misunderstood as prediction or description, when it intends to evoke and generate an alternative horizon about the future that will bring to an end present (unwitting?) policies and practices that are inimical to the rule of God. The scrolls that are to be opened are from "elsewhere," that is, from the mystery of God's own rule. They are "sealed" because the present regime of defiance (with its well-contained logic) can have no access to the disclosure. Indeed the only access given to the substance of the sealed scrolls is to those who disengage from and resist present imperial rule that contradicts the intent of God.

II.

As we focus on Rev 8:1 we may consider the material before that cosmic moment of silence (6:1—7:17) and the material that comes after that verse (8:2—9:21). The material before our verse consists in two parts. First there is the opening of the first six scrolls. Because we know that the writer (visionary!) is committed to a series of "sevens," we know that the first six scrolls are preliminary to the primary seventh assertion of the reckoning. In these six scrolls we have the appearance of "living creatures" who are carriers of death (see 6:8). The outcome of their appearance is the ending of the present order of creation. Present world arrangements constitute a pretend-order that is in fact chaos. The text does not bother here to give reasons for that divine judgment. The reasons will be given later that bespeak autonomy, arrogance, and violent exploitation that constitute the policies of "Babylon," that is, Rome.[1] The empire embraces chaos that defies the given order of creation and its end is not good.

But second in the sequence of the text, the process of opening the seals of the scrolls is instigated by an angel who becomes the voice of "the living God." That is, we have interpretation by a messenger from God who speaks a word for God. That speaking concerns the "living God" (7:2), the one who has energy, power, and will in contrast to the gods of the empire who in fact have no capacity for life.

In the midst of the devastation declared in the first six scrolls, there is this commanding presence of the living God who is not finally reduced to the fate decreed in the scrolls, even though the scrolls come from this God. God can and does speak even outside of and beyond the scrolls. The living God places a momentary "hold" on the process and enactment of divine judgment. That judgment, it is recognized, will be a wholesale

---

1. See Davis, *Biblical Prophecy*, 127-33.

environmental disaster; the disobedience of the empire brings judgment not only on the empire but upon the world it inhabits. The judgment, however, is not total:

> Do not damage the earth or the sea or the trees, until we have marked the servants of our God with a seal on their foreheads. (7:3)

The "until" of God means a delay, so that the faithful can be marked in a way that will exempt them from the total devastation. The one protected and exempted are "sealed," as the church declares in baptism, "sealed as Christ's own forever."

What follows in the midst of the anticipated devastation is that those protected and exempted are enumerated tribe by tribe in perfect symmetry, so that the faithful from all Israel constitute the protected remnant (7:4–8). The vision concerns a restoration of faithful Israel. The roll call of the protected is reminiscent of the perfect symmetry of Ezek 47:13—48:29 that anticipates a well ordered restoration of Israel in the new restored Jerusalem. These verses of restoration in both texts, Ezekiel and Revelation, override the messiness and confusion of historical reality and instead offer a picture of a properly ordered world presided over by the majestic creator who intends a world order of wellbeing. The entire scene is an affirmation of the rule of God to protect and exempt those who have been faithful in the midst of imperial defiance.

Because these properly ordered faithful anticipate a good future, they are the ones who have come through the "great ordeal" (Rev 7:14). The "ordeal," in the horizon of the writer, concerns those who have confessed Christ and who have thereby defied Rome and refused the claims of the empire. They are the ones who did not shrink from the cost of their faith, and who did not doubt the truth of the Gospel and the future to be given to those who lived out the gospel.

When we consider "the great ordeal" cast in such imagery, we have to translate it into our own circumstance that, as in ancient Rome, concerns the domination of an imperial system of scarcity-greed-violence that has become "normal" in our practice of military consumerism. If we read with such contemporaneity, the "faithful" are the ones who see the falseness of the greed system that has become normal and who, by their way of living, defy the dominant system and live faithfully otherwise. In many parts of the world that defiance of the dominant system is exceedingly costly. It is less costly (so far!) in our own society, but it is not without cost.

III. The Riddle of Silence and Speech

It is no wonder that those who came through "the great ordeal" without compromise, even when they have suffered, are ready and able to engage in exuberant doxology, singing to the God whom they have trusted and obeyed at great risk (7:12, 15–17). The doxology in v. 12 strikes the cadence of the ancient Psalter. It asserts, in a torrent of laud, that all honor and power belong to God, and not to the claims of Caesar. All—the angels, the elders, and the living creatures—gladly abase themselves before the divine majesty (7:11). The act of doxology is substantively a yielding in gladness to God; functionally it serves to enhance the rule of God in a way that diminishes and dismisses the rule of Caesar and the Roman gods.

That conventional Psalmic cadence, however, is clearly modified in vv. 15–17 by an assertion that it is *the Lamb* who is the target of glad worship:

> After this I looked and there was a great multitude that no one could count, from every nation, from all tribes and peoples and tongues, standing before the throne and before *the Lamb,* robed in white, with palm branches in their hands (v. 9).

> For *the Lamb* at the center of the throne will be their shepherd,
>   and he will guide them to springs of the water of life
>   and God will wipe away every tear from their eyes. (v. 17)

The centrality of *the Lamb* decisively alters and refocuses the praise of Israel. Jesus, the Paschal Lamb, has been victimized by the power of the empire. Thus the rhetoric is an allusion to the *crucifixion of Jesus* at the hands of the empire; that he is the object of doxology affirms the *resurrection of Jesus* to lordly power. Thus the doxologies of Israel are recast as glad acknowledgement of "the mystery of faith" that "Christ has died, Christ is risen." This "mystery" is an assertion that the power of Rome has been overcome. Jesus' execution by the empire was designed to eliminate him and his movement, but the empire could not make it stick. Those who are "sealed as Christ's own" are those have been through the great ordeal and are marked for protection; they can do nothing but engage in endless praise to the creator God who rules. They refuse the silence of the empire.

Their praise, moreover, is a celebration of a new creation that is displacing the old imperial claims. In that new governance, there is no more hunger or thirst; there is no more killing heat (from global warming?) (v. 16). In place of such bodily threats there is now the "water of life" and the end of tears (v. 17). The language of v. 17 is of course an allusion to Psalm 23 and to the promise of Ezekiel 34. Through the person of Jesus, the doxology affirms, God is the giver of new life as promised in the old tradition:

> I myself will search for my sheep, and will seek them out. As shepherds seek out their flocks when they are among their scattered sheep, so I will seek out my sheep. I will rescue them from all the places to which they have been scattered on a day of cloud and thick darkness . . . I will feed them with good pasture, and the mountain heights of Israel will be their pasture; there they shall lie down in good grazing land, and they shall feed on rich pasture on the mountains of Israel. I myself will be the shepherd of my sheep, and I will make them lie down, says the Lord God. I will seek the lost, and I will bring back the strayed, and I will bind up the injured, and I will strengthen the weak. (Ezek 34:11–16a).

The divine resolve ends this way:

> But the fat and the strong I will destroy. I will feed them with justice. (v. 16b)

The "fat and strong" are the practitioners of injustice; their reign will end! The text invites the assumption and affirmation that present powers of domination are failed powers that do not merit allegiance, obedience, or respect. Thus the doxology in our verses celebrates the end of unjust governance and emancipation by the liberating God. This singing itself is an act of defiant emancipation. Thus the sum of Rev 7:1–17 is an interruption of the sweeping bad news of the sealed scrolls. This interruption of good news is for those who have decided otherwise for the sake of the One who has given the scrolls of the future.

III.

We do not need to linger long over the material that follows our verse in 8:2—9:21. The disclosure of the seventh seal is all bad news for the present dominant system. The target of the bad news is not individual persons in that regime, but the entire socio-political system and its environmental context that is an enactment of enormous hubris. The coming disaster of the dominant regime is underwritten by the rule and order of the creator God who will not be mocked. That future for the defiant regime is already written in the scroll!

IV.

Our verse, Rev 8:1, is dramatically situated. By this time we have finished with the first six sealed scrolls (6:1–17) and with the interruption of doxology by the protected and exempted (7:1–17). We know that there will be a seventh scroll that will be ominous and certain. No wonder there is a dramatic pause like a deep breath before we go further. In the silence that was long (perhaps because "a thousand ages in your sight are like an evening gone"),[2] the cadence of doxology surely continued to echo and ring in the ears of the angels in heaven and the errant regime on earth. The six seals, the great ordeal, and the eruption of doxology for the Lamb set the dramatic either/or in the most intense way.

Now there is silence.[3] The voice that gave expression to the wrath of the seals has stopped. We know there will be a seventh seal, but not yet. The marked ones had sung their lungs out in praise, and now they are stopped as well. The angels stopped and the trumpets stopped. There was utter silence in heaven, and earth had no more to say.

This is an instant that is reserved for the Lamb alone, the one silenced and now empowered. It is a moment of awe before inexpressible holiness, a presence and a governance that fits none of our conventional categories and that accommodates none of our "normal" expectations. It is a pause in which to ponder the either/or that is the theme of the entire book of Revelation. There is the either of the old world dominated by exploitation and commoditization, and the "or" of the Lamb that is a world of vulnerability to the neighbor. We do not need to speak in this moment, and must not speak. The either/or occupies the divine pause that occurs in the midst of a pyro-technical drama. The either/or is acutely here and now. The "world" that is under judgment is the world of domination. The world to come is a political economy of neighborly generosity. We know that from the witness of the Lamb. The final verses of the doxology in 7:16–17 anticipate the new world. It will be a world of ample food for all ("hunger no more") and free pure water ("thirst no more"; see Isa 55:1–2). The tears of exploitation, displacement, and oppression no more . . . no more stratification that breeds inequality. In this dramatic instant of silence the entire creation of heaven

---

2. These famous words are from Watts, "O God Our Help in Ages Past."

3. As noted above, the only other use of this term for "silence" in the New Testament is in Acts 21:40. It will be interesting and suggestive to consider the interplay between these two uses, both of which concern attestation to Jesus as the Messiah.

and earth is "taking time to be holy," taking time to reckon with the daily practice of life or death in the presence of God.

After the thirty seconds that was long enough to adjudicate this grand either/or, the silence is broken. It is broken by the seven trumpets that announce the settled future of a failed world (8:3ff.). There follows after these trumpets "from elsewhere" fire, hail, blood, wormwood, and a darkness that comes to "woe, woe, woe" (8:13). Then come a bottomless pit, torture, the sting of scorpions, locust and death. The voice with the trumpets breaks the silence with dire danger.

The silence was also broken by the resumption of doxology. The seventh angel blew the trumpet. And then this:

> The kingdom of the world has become the kingdom of our Lord
> and of *his Messiah*,
> and he will reign forever. (11:15)

We may imagine a contest between these voices of death and the voice of thanks, one voice to terminate what has failed, one voice to celebrate the arrival of the rule of the Lamb. Or perhaps it is a convergence of voices, for the threat to the old order given in the scrolls and the joyous anticipation by the marked ones of the newness to come arrive in the same instant. The silence could not last longer than thirty seconds because the rule of God, in a panoply of new gifts, requires speech and song. But both *the scrolls of judgment* and *the songs of thanks* are evoked by that instant of awed silence in which the holiness of the Lamb is the overwhelming reality before which all creation must pause in stunned acknowledgement.

IV.

It occurs to me that this awed silence before the Lamb is a compelling antipode to the text with which we began our study, Hab 2:20. Both of these texts feature silence in awe before the holy God. The decisive contrast, however, concerns the God acknowledged in these two silences. Here in Rev 8:1 the silence is before the Lamb who was slain and governs in power. The power of the Lamb, however, cannot be confused with the power of the empire of Rome. Indeed, the power of the Lamb contrasts with the power of Rome and its gods, for the Lamb specializes in neighborly justice and a peaceable governance without the imposition of tears or violence. The one who occupies the silence in our text is very different from God who

III. The Riddle of Silence and Speech

occupies the temple in Hab 2:20. The temple in Jerusalem as the citadel of the Davidic-Solomonic kingdom, a kingdom of confiscation, commoditization, and exploitation, that is, of power exercised in aggressive ways.[4] The temple and its occupying God constituted a practice and legitimation of a "worldly" regime. The silence commended by the priests in Hab 2:20 was awe before worldly power. By contrast the silence observed in our text concerns the God (Lamb) who contradicts the power of the world. This silence is submission to a very different authority who is narrated on Friday and Sunday.

This latter silence (thirty seconds!!) is indeed "apocalyptic" silence. That is, it is silence that "reveals" and "discloses" a holy reality that is discontinuous from all of our conventional categories. It is most unfortunate "apocalyptic" has been distorted by science-fiction dramatics. In fact this literature is an attempt to put before us not a cataclysm, but an either/or about which we must decide. It would have been moving to get God's new world in the pyro-violence of Mel Gibson, but that is to misunderstand the imagery. The drama puts before us the "either/or," either to be summoned by the trumpets for termination; or to be included among the singers who enter the new world initiated by the Lamb. This either/or is not escape into an unreal world. Nor is it engagement in violence. It is rather life in obedience when bread is shared where there is no hunger and water is shared where there is no thirst, and justice is practiced where there are no tears. It is a world order that moves gladly away from environmental disaster so readily sponsored by empire. The glad doxologies are sung by those who have come down where they ought to be, in the company of the Lamb:

> See, the home of God is among morals.
> He will dwell with them;
> they will be his peoples,
> and God himself will be with them;
> he will wipe every tear from their eyes.
> Death will be no more;
> mourning and crying and pain will be no more,
> for the first things have passed away. (Rev 21:3–4).

No more Death! It does not require more than thirty seconds to decide, in this awed silence, that this is the gift of life apart from the empire that traffics in death. It is no wonder that the final prayer of those who have signed on with the Lamb is "'Come, Lord Jesus!" The coming of that new rule is

---

4. See Brueggemann, *Solomon*, 87–103 and *passim*.

never too soon for those who are marked, who come out of the silence with a clear confession and a faithful practice.

15

Divine Speech via Silence

But the LORD was not in the wind; and after the wind an earthquake, but the LORD was not in the earthquake; and after the earthquake a fire, but the LORD as not in the fire; and after the fire a sound of sheer silence. (1 Kgs 19:11–12)

THE NARRATIVE OF 1 Kgs 19:1–18 is thick with visitation. In v. 5 an angel feeds Elijah. In v. 13 a voice speaks. And all through the narrative, there is YHWH, the God of Horeb (Sinai) who is variously silent or speaking, absent or present. These several visitations put us on notice that this is no ordinary story that can be parsed through our conventional imagination. This is, rather, a narrative in which the holiness of God is decisively at play, albeit in hidden ways.

I.

The story reminisces about "theophany." This is a term that combines *theos* (God) and *phany* (manifest), thus a "manifestation of God." In ancient biblical narrative, theophany is a stylized report that features the dramatic, even catastrophic eruption of God, what we might call "heavenly fireworks." Such narratives often attest earthquakes, powerful wind, dangerous fire, plus trumpet sounds from on high, all of which are said to accompany of God's awesome, dangerous entry into human experience. The classic case in the Old Testament the theophany of God at Mt. Sinai in Exod 19:16–25 that situates God among thunder, lightning, smoke, earthquake, and a blast of trumpet. We have an echo of such appearance in Hab 3:3–15.

In important ways the Elijah narrative seems to echo that of Moses. In the contest at Mt. Carmel we have traces of the same narrative "fireworks" that leads to an acknowledgment of YHWH as Lord:

> The fire of the LORD fell and consumed the burnt offering, the wood, the stones, and the dust, and even licked up the water that was in the trench. When all the people saw it, they fell on their faces and said, "The LORD indeed is God; the LORD indeed is God." (1 Kgs 18:38–39)

Now in our narrative there is expectation of like divine presence. Elijah is commanded to go and stand in the mountain (19:11). The mountain, moreover, is Horeb (elsewhere called "Sinai"), that is, the mountain of Moses. More than that, YHWH proposes to "pass by" just as YHWH's glory "passed by" Moses (Exod 33:21–23). The parallel phrasing indicates that there is an intentional allusion back to the Moses encounter.

And indeed there was a great wind. That wind, however, did not amount to a theophany; the wind was followed by the upheaval of earthquake and then by fire ... all the markings of theophany. But, we are told, none these dramatic forces contained YHWH. Three times we are told "not": not in the wind, not in the earthquake, not in the fire. It is *phany*, but no *theos*. God was not packaged in such ferocious occurrences. The absence of God from these dramatic vehicles, perhaps attests to new experience for the prophet. Or perhaps it is designed to protect the singularity of Moses whom Elijah cannot rival. Samuel Terrien judges that the narrative indicates a transition: "Between the *legenda* of the presence in historical events and the historical sobriety of the records of the great prophets, for whom presence is individualized, interiorized, and often curtailed or adumbrated."[1] And from this Terrien concludes: "Elijah was not a new Moses. He became the forerunner of Amos."[2] Or in much more puckish mood, Karl Barth can judge that such dramatic encounter does not in fact change anything:

> If any one has been changed in these years, it is certainly not in virtue of the extraordinary situations into which they have led him. According to the present trend, we may suppose that even on the

---

1. Terrien, *The Elusive Presence*, 234.
2. Terrien, *The Elusive Presence*, 236.

III. The Riddle of Silence and Speech

morning after the Day of Judgment—if such a thing were possible- every cabaret, every night club, every newspaper firm eager for advertisements and subscriptions, every nest of political fanatics, every pagan discussions group, indeed, every Christian tea-party an Church synod would resume business to the best of its ability, and with a new sense of opportunity, completely unmoved, quite uninstructed, and in no serious sense different from what it was before. Fire, drought, earthquake, war, pestilence, the darkness of the sun and similar phenomena are not things to plunge us into real anguish, and therefore to give us real peace. The LORD was not in the storm, the earthquake or the fire. (1 Kg. 19:11f.) He really was not.[3]

The narrative has ample "fireworks." They are not, however, any longer marked as "heavenly." Wind, earthquake, and fire are no adequate vehicles for the presence of God.

II.

What then? Well then, silence! The silence is after all of the spectacles that witness to no God. The phrasing used in v. 12 is familiarly "a still small voice." That translation, however, is an attempt to lessen the silence of God's holiness. Thus the NRSV has it much better: "the sound of sheer silence." The actual phase is a "voice muted" (not muted like a saxophone, but actual muteness). Thus Marvin Sweeney can see that the terms offer a dramatic contradiction: "The term *qol*, "sound" and *demama*, "silence" contradict each other in a metaphorical presentation of power through a combination of presence and absence."[4]

Elijah is here in the presence of holiness that is withheld from him, but no less present to him. The Bible, as we say, is "God's word" and "God's word" is uttered and we confess has "become flesh." But here, in this dramatic moment, that word is withheld and unuttered, so that Elijah and all who attend to this text are compelled to see that this voice is like none other, because it is mute, and this muteness is like none other because it is voiced. Try as we will, the phrase cannot be decoded. God has promised Elijah to "pass by" as God "passed by" Moses. Moses saw no form; and now Elijah "hears no voice," except a voice that defies our categories.

---

3. Barth, *Church Dogmatics* III/2, 115.
4. Sweeney, *I & II Kings*, 232.

II.

Strangely (or perhaps fortunately), the story does not end there. In v. 12 Elijah is obedient. He has been commanded to "stand on the mountain," and he does, just as Moses had done. The first word in v. 13 can be translated "When he heard" as in the NRSV, or it can be "as he listened." Either way, he is obedient; he listened to a voice that is mute. Except that the voice was not mute in v. 11 when it issued a command. One can see that the narrative itself is quite unsettled about the matter of speech and silence. In any case Elijah is obedient, willing to wait and to listen. It is a dangerous wait. He has a coat over his face, lest he see too much, or perhaps lest he hear too much. His coat, however, will not protect him from the voice of muteness that now addresses him and calls him by name (v. 13).

III.

Now that Elijah is in place as he has been commanded, the mute voice breaks the muteness. A voice came to him! No more silence! Now it is an address that amounts to a summons. Elijah is interrogated: "What are you doing here? Hiding in a cave?" Or perhaps "What are you doing waiting at the entrance of the cave?" Perhaps it is a question that anticipates John the Baptizer, "What did you come out to see?" (Matt 11:7–9). What were you expecting? One senses that it is a reprimand. Elijah responds in self-defense:

> I have been very zealous for the LORD, the God of hosts; for the Israelites have forsaken your covenant, thrown down your altars, and killed your prophets with the sword. I alone am left, and they are seeking my life, to take it away. (v. 14)

It is very dangerous out there! They are killing people like me! I have been utterly faithful and have run great risks for YHWH. I have done so in a recalcitrant society that violates covenant, that cares not at all for the God of covenant or for the messenger of that God. Perhaps Elijah is a bit incredulous that YHWH is so ill-informed that YHWH would not understand why Elijah is hiding out.

But that justification by Elijah will not be credited by YHWH. The divine response simply ignores his self-protective stance. Terrien observes of this exchange:[5]

---

5. Terrien, *The Elusive Presence*, 234–36.

III. The Riddle of Silence and Speech

a) The God who "passes by" is on the move:
He never ceases from going and coming. In a manner of speaking, his absence is never far from his presence, and silence precedes the hearing of his word ... When silence comes, however, and when man truly hears it and enters into the proper attitude of theocentric worship, God speaks.

b) This God is not the one Elijah expected.

c) This God makes a response that is highly contextual to the religious crisis of the moment, namely, the seductions of Baal that now propel the toxic policies of the crown.

The voice that now speaks, no longer mute, responds as though Elijah had not said anything. This voice has no interest in Elijah's personal plight and no symphony for his danger or his fear. The response of God is not unlike the response of God in the whirlwind to the complaints of Job (Job 38:1). It may be intentionally ironic that in the response to Job, God speaks from the whirlwind, perhaps the wind from which God was absent for Elijah.

In any case, the response to Elijah is an imperative: "Go!" (v. 15). Get out of the cave. Disregard your fear. Never mind the risk. The holy God insists, in completely unaccommodating terms, upon an agenda that is massive and risky. Elijah is summoned to disregard himself and get on with the assignment. His work is three times to "anoint," that is, to commit a highly freighted, subversive symbolic act that contradicts all things conventional. The mandate is not unlike that of Samuel when he is commanded to anoint David as king, a command that Samuel recognizes to be a high risk (1 Sam 16:1–2).

First, Elijah is to designate a new king in Syria (Aram); this is an act of treason to the present king who is committed to Baal. It is astonishing that Elijah's mandate is beyond the confines of Israel, into a zone where we did not know that YHWH had a vested interest. Second, Elijah is to designate a new king in Israel who will terminate the present dynasty of Omri (and Ahab) that had been vigorously committed to Baal and the anti-covenantal, anti-neighborly economics that stem from Baal. Thus the divine oracle envisions an overthrow of royal regimes that are well situated in conventional politics. The third act to which Elijah is summoned is the designation of Elisha "as a prophet in your place." This third assignment may seem more benign, a prophet, not the overthrow of a royal regime. Except that in v. 17

YHWH provides a sequence of killings that Elisha will complete, so that the divine command envisions a massive disruption of royal history, nothing less than the delegitimation and termination of royal power that has run amok.

Almost as a throw-away line, v. 18 offers a belated assurance that indirectly (finally!) acknowledges the fears that Elijah had voiced in v. 14. Now this voice that breaks silence and speaks offers an assurance to Elijah that he is not, as he mistakenly thought, the only one left. There is still a strong company of the faithful who have not sold out to Baalism. Elijah is not alone, but belongs to a steadfast company. YHWH is not defeated, but is ready for a new offensive. YHWH will not retreat to a cave for safety; and neither must Elijah!

IV.

Given our theme of silence, our interest is in that odd inexplicable instant when *the voice of muteness* becomes *the voice of mandate* and then, belatedly, *the voice of assurance*. It is as though the muteness were a moment of reticence in which the speaking God is consolidating energy and will for a new initiative. When we have romantically rendered this defining phrase as "a still small voice," we have characteristically stopped reading at v. 12, or at best we have permitted Elijah to answer in v. 14 with his complaint, but not more than that. We have not been inclined to read further, because the reported mandates that follow push us well beyond our comfort zone of "religious reading."

If, however, we consider the rest of the encounter, we may look more closely at what this voice (mute and then speaking) does. The muteness gets the attention of Elijah and the rest of us as belated readers. We are put on notice that this is holiness on the loose. And when the silence is broken, what the voice does is to *authorize human agency*. It is as though this hiddenness plants a seed of responsibility and possibility. The rest is human action, much of which—according to plan-is violent public activity. This combination of *divine authorization* and *human performance* is characteristic of biblical narrative. It has been so since the exodus. In Exod 3:7–9 YHWH voices all kinds of promises and resolves. But then in v. 10, it is Moses, not YHWH, who must go to Pharaoh. Over a lifetime of study Terence Fretheim has helped me to see this calculus at work in the biblical text. God's legitimating action is crucial; but the action is entrusted to human agency. God does not do the heavy lifting. That is human work. Indeed, one could see that this linkage and sequence of *divine authorization* and *human performance* is exactly what the church confesses in "truly God, truly human" when the two sides of the transaction converge. And in our own time, we may judge that extraordinary things have happened in our history because *human agents* have been and known themselves to be *divinely authorized*. The most obvious instance in our recent time is Martin Luther King Jr. Clearly King was and knew himself to be divinely authorized, quite specifically authorized by a "voice" in his kitchen experience.[6] Clearly King had to run all the risks, compelled by that voice. He discovered, moreover, that there were seven thousand companions who had not bowed the knee. The point of contestation, then as now, is that muted voice that speaks.

V.

Here are three derivative reflections:

First, it is clear that this narrative is plunge into historical risk propelled by divine legitimation. We may not read the voice of sheer silence ("still small voice") in any way as romanticized or privatized. The narrative is aimed toward historical specificity of an urgent kind. The work of Elijah, and of Elisha after him, is to delegitimate rulers who have in principle forfeited their claim to authority. It is the risky work of delegitimation, the kind of work that Jesus undertakes in his trial before Pilate, or as Paul Lehmann has it, of Pilate's trial before Jesus.[7]

Second, the presence of "7,000" is an assurance of a "remnant," as the term "leave" in v. 18 is in fact a remnant-evoking word. Terrien sees this sub-community as

> A community of the faithful which could survive the destruction of the state and the annihilation of cultus, and which could potentially explode the restrictiveness of an ethnic community. Here we witness the birth of the idea of *ecclesia*, an assembly of those who

---

6. Dr. King reported that after the bombing of his house on January 27, 1956, he sat alone and desolate that night in his kitchen. He reported: "It seemed at that moment, I could hear an inner voice saying to me, "Martin Luther, stand up for righteousness. Stand up for justice. Stand up for truth. And lo, I will be with you, even until the end of the world." His statement has been quoted in many venues. See Dear, "Back to Home."

7. Lehmann, *The Transfiguration of Politics*, 48–70.

trust their God rather than submit to the tyranny of political or institutional conformism.⁸

Of course this is not the institutional church of Christendom that all too much has "bowed down and kissed" the gods of commodity. It is, however, an assurance and an anticipation of a faithful community.

In his careful delineation of the Jesus movement as an embodiment of that faithful remnant, Paul cites the protest of Elijah and the divine response to that protest (Rom 11:2–3). Paul's exposition of the faithful remnant is that it is a community "chosen by grace" (v. 5). In this exposition Paul is not sloganeering about a "theology of grace," but is attending to the conviction that in the midst of principalities and powers there is and can be such an alternative community that acts out the truth. In our present practice of faith, we may be grateful for a voice of sheer silence that has authorized risk-taking in the midst of empires that specialize in "bowing to and kissing."⁹

Third, we are in this text at the "end of theophany" when there is no "heavenly" to the "fireworks of wind, earthquake and fire. We may reflect critically on the eagerness of our society for a "religious experience," or even more for the prospects of "spiritual experience" as though the holy God were readily "on call." Such a thirst for "spirituality" treats "religious truth "as though it were a salve and a comfort in the midst of status quo living that goes unchallenged. This text, reflective of the dominant propensity of the Bible, makes the claim that the true God of the gospel characteristically comes not as comfort but as mandate. Thus the abrupt "go" issued in 19:15 is a recurring imperative in gospel faith. Jurgen Moltmann, in his programmatic insistence, has seen that in the modern world we are variously tempted to "The Cult of the Absolute," "The Cult of the 'New Subjectivity,'" the "Cult of 'Co-humanity,'" and the "Cult of 'the Institution.'"¹⁰ Moltmann's exposition is worth careful study in light of our text. Each of these "cults" that Moltmann identifies is amounts to accommodation to status quo empire that leads away from missional mandate. Theophany is endlessly seductive; sheer silence, by contrast issues in vocation.

Albeit with music that is much too romantic, we do sing in recognition of the dangers of "theophany":

---

8. Terrien, *The Elusive Presence*, 233–34.
9. I use the term "empire" with a nuance of irony as suggested by White, *Living Speech*.
10. Moltmann, *Theology of Hope*, 304–24.

III. The Riddle of Silence and Speech

> I ask no dream, no prophet ecstasies,
> no sudden rending of the veil of clay,
> no angel visitant, no opening skies,
> but take the dimness of my soul away.[11]

Theophany contained in the status quo results in "dimness of soul." Sheer silence propels elsewhere. Its call it is risky, to be sure. But a goodly company of companions makes the imperative as viable as it is urgent.

---

11. Croly, "Spirit of God, Descend upon My Heart."

IV

The Landscape of Jeremiah's Sojourn
Four Studies in the Book of Jeremiah

16

The Sermon

Jeremiah 7:1-15

THE PROPHET JEREMIAH WAS called, against his will, to speak the truth in down-town Jerusalem (Jer 1:4-10). He was situated, throughout his long ministry, in the midst of Jerusalem's most acute historical crisis (609-581 BCE). During his ministry, in 587 BCE, the holy city of Jerusalem would be destroyed, the temple burned, and the Davidic king exiled. Everyone could see that the destruction and deportation were caused by the Babylonian army under Nebuchadnezzar. But Jeremiah's mandate was more difficult than that. It was his work to assert that the Babylonian army had come against Jerusalem at the behest of YHWH, the God of the covenant. The destruction, moreover, was because God was punishing Jerusalem for its long, serious violation of the covenant of Mt. Sinai. Thus the destruction of the city was in fact an unfolding of the conditions of Israel's covenant with YHWH.

In the early chapters of Jeremiah, the prophet speaks poetry in order to exhibit the broken covenant with YHWH that is the source of all the problems to come for the city. The prophet uses bold imagery in order to penetrate the ideological façade of Jerusalem and to help the residents of the city to see what is in fact happening before their very eyes that they did not yet see. He speaks of violated love (3:2), of broken cisterns (2:13), of an invading army (4:19-20), and the dismantling of all creation (4:23-26), all images for the loss about to be experienced in Jerusalem that they did not yet anticipate.

IV. The Landscape of Jeremiah's Sojourn

Jeremiah's task, given in his call, is to "pluck up and break down, to destroy and overthrow" (1:10). He does this by his imaginative rhetoric whereby he challenges the assumptions and unquestioned ideology of his establishment listeners. Finally, all of this comes together in his famous "temple sermon" that occupies the defining place in the early chapters of the book (7:1–15). (It is likely that the verses that follow (vv. 16–34) are commentary added later to the sermon.)

—The sermon is mandated by God and delivered in the courtyard of the temple, a place sure to draw a crowd (vv. 1–2).

—The sermon calls for "amendment," that is, for a radical change in the attitude, practices, and policy of the residents in the city, not least the royal dynasty and the temple priests (v. 3).

—The prophet mocks the self-confident mantra of the community, whether it is a liturgical formula or a spasm of self-deceiving patriotism: "The temple of the LORD, the temple of the LORD . . ." (v. 4).

—As an alternative to smug reliance on such ideological mantras, the prophet proposes changed practices toward the marginal and vulnerable in society, the immigrant, orphans, and widows. These are the ones who have no resources or advocates, so that the community itself is responsible for their well-being (vv. 5–7). These verses are governed by a series of "ifs" followed in v. 7 by a "then." The "if-then" pattern of speech shows that everything is conditional and depends upon Israel's right social action in obedience to the commands of the covenant.

—In vv. 8–11, the prophet taunts his self-deceiving listeners. He accuses them of: a) violating the Ten Commandments; and then b) coming to the temple as a safe haven. That the temple has become a "den of robbers" suggests it serves as a "safe house" for high class "legal" criminals, the ones who prey upon the vulnerable in society. Religion has become a cover for exploitative social policy and practice.

—As a "sermon illustration," the prophet compares Jerusalem, the holy city, to the ancient shrine of Shiloh (vv. 12–15). In former times, still remembered, Shiloh has been a prominent place of religious pilgrimage (see 1 Sam 1:1). But then the shrine and the city were destroyed and left forever in ruins. This would have been known in Jerusalem. The comparison dared to suggest that Jerusalem is subject to the same threat, if it does not change its policy and its practices. No doubt the ancients in Shiloh had assumed they were guaranteed protection by God as a special shrine, as folk in Jerusalem assumed in the time of Jeremiah. The prophetic word is that no one, not even God's special people or God's special city, gets a "pass" from the God of justice who wants the vulnerable cared for. The final sentence concerning "cast out" in v. 15 is an allusion to exile and deportation, a common threat in that ancient world, and a recurring theme in Jeremiah that was about to be the experience of the holy city and its residents.

Note well that the harsh rhetoric of this sermon contradicts the common assumptions of the city, the king, and the temple. It challenged the consensus conviction that Jerusalem would always be kept safe by God, and affirmed that such protection by God depends upon faithful covenant keeping. As it turned out, the threat voiced in the sermon was serious and substantive; the eventual experience of Jerusalem, still in the life-time of Jeremiah, was indeed one of destruction, loss, and deportation. The sermon turned out to be an act of truth-telling in a city that did not welcome such truthfulness.

QUESTIONS FOR DISCUSSION

1. What would it be like to hear such a sermon in privileged Jerusalem in that time?
2. What would it require of Jeremiah to be able to speak these demanding words?
3. How do you think such a sermon would sound now in the United States?
4. What changes in policy or practice might be required among us in response to such a sermon?
5. What illusions can you identify that we trust in today?
6. Can you identify some voices among us who sound like Jeremiah? Do we need some?

17

The Trial

Jeremiah 26:1–19, 24

JEREMIAH'S SAVAGE RHETORIC ABOUT the coming threat against Jerusalem continues through the first half of the book He critiques the most "sacred cows" of his society, the kingship of David and the religious leadership.

Against the monarch that is grounded in the unconditional divine promise of 2 Sam 7:1–16, Jeremiah attacks the rule of Jehoiachim, son of Josiah, who reigned from 609 to 598 BCE (see 2 Kgs 23:36—24:7). He accuses the king of "injustice and unrighteousness" by exploiting cheap labor for the sake of his extravagant building program (Jer 22:13–14). By using these two words of condemnation, the prophet appeals to the oldest imperatives of the covenant. He anticipates, moreover, that such a self-serving king will die an ignoble death without any proper grievance by his subjects (Jer 22:18–19). In vv. 28–30, he grieves the next king, Jehoiachin (Coniah), who will be "cast away" into a foreign land (see 2 Kgs 24:8–12). More generally Jeremiah declares a judgment against the "shepherds" (kings) who have "scattered my flock," that is, caused Israel to go into exile (Jer 23:1–2; see Ezek 34:1–10). Thus he judges that the kings, taken all together, are an utter failure. Their assignment was to enhance the life of the people; but just the opposite has been accomplished.

In like manner he condemns the prophets who are allied with establishment power and who echo the party line (Jer 23:9–22). H judges that they are "ungodly" and "wicked," regularly uttering false words that do not

The Trial

derive from the will of YHWH, thereby helping to seduce and mislead the people into false life.

It is no wonder that in chapter 26, mid-point in the book, Jeremiah is brought to trial as an enemy of the people. (In 38:4, he is called a traitor). Verses 1–6 connect the narrative report that follows to the sermon of chapter 7. The reference to Shiloh in v. 6 echoes the earlier comparison. It is asserted that the divine purpose of the sermon in chapter 7 was to cause the people to "turn . . . change their mind . . . listen" and walk in the way of the Torah. The latter likely refers to the Torah of the book of Deuteronomy with its accent on "widow, orphan, and immigrant" (see Deut 24:17–22). Jeremiah thus had summoned Israel back to its foundational commitments of covenant. For that he is summoned into court, because the "priests and prophets," the religious leadership, were affronted by his words that dared to expose the establishment (26:7–10). They brought capital charges against him: "You shall die!" being especially offended by his comparison of Jerusalem with Shiloh that had been devastated.

In vv. 10–11, the charge brought by the "priests and prophets" is heard by the civil officials, that is, the judiciary. Jeremiah is given opportunity to offer his own defense which he does in two parts. First, in vv. 12–13, he focuses on his prophetic message that is given by God and that calls Jerusalem to listen and repent. Indeed, he allows that the coming devastation of the city can be averted if there is genuine repentance. Second, he shifts attention for a moment away from his message to his person (v. 14). But in fact he makes no self-defense. He submits himself willingly to the court, only to declare that if he is executed, it will be a costly death of an innocent man, thus shedding "innocent blood" (v. 15). That is, he is innocent because he is mandated by God to speak the truth.

The verdict of the court is offered in vv. 16–19. The civic officials, against the religious leadership, concluded that Jeremiah cannot be executed for critiquing the establishment, because his word is a word from YHWH. The supportive argument for the verdict comes from an unexpected source, "elders of the land." These are country people who attended the trial and who could recall the words of the prophet Micah a century earlier. Because they cite Micah, it is probable that they come from his home territory of Gath southwest of Jerusalem. In v. 18, they recall quite specifically the older prophetic utterance from Mic 3:12. This is a remarkable case in which an older biblical source is cited by the Bible itself, a quote that functions as a legal precedent in the trial. The argument is that a word of judgment against the establishment and its ideology is appropriately spoken, if it is rooted in God's own purpose. The argument makes room for a theological-moral critique of establishment ideology, so that the establishment ideology cannot be a closed system that is immune to critique.

We are not told how the trial ended. It is, however, reported that v. 24 that a son of Shaphan stood with Jeremiah and so protected him from both official execution and informal lynching. We know from elsewhere in the book of Jeremiah that Shaphan and his family were powerful political operators in Jerusalem who stood opposed to the self-defeating policies of the royal establishment. This means on the one hand that Jeremiah had powerful political connections; on the other hand, it means that he was a spokesperson for a considerable public opinion that opposed the "exceptionalism" of throne and temple in Jerusalem. This body of opinion believed that adherence to covenant and not posturing policy was a way toward survival. This is a sort of political realism that refuses the cant of popular political opinion. We are able to see in Jeremiah a convergence of faith and politics in which truth protests against a practice of power that is self-deceptive and illusionary. In the next two chapters of the book, Jeremiah's "yoke" points to the coming of Babylon that will reduce Jerusalem to an impotent subordinate colony (Jer 27–28). For Jeremiah that public humiliation of the city is evidence of YHWH's will and purpose.

QUESTIONS FOR DISCUSSION

1. What do you think of the resolve of the religious leaders who want to silence a dangerous poet?

2. How would you imagine the "country elders" who cite old precedents in order to protect the prophet?

3. Can you imagine a trial in our society where established power tries to silence uncomfortable truth?

4. Do you see parallels between the trial of Jeremiah in this text and the trial of Jesus as reported in John 18:28—19:16?

5. What image of Shaphan do you get from this narrative? Can you identify any political players in our time who might protect a truth-speaking voice?

18

The Covenant

Jeremiah 31:31-34

EARLY ON, JEREMIAH HAD been an advocate of the covenant of Sinai, likely in context a reference to the covenant in Deuteronomy (see Deut 5:3): "Hear the words of this covenant, and speak to the inhabitants of Jerusalem . . . So you shall be my people, and I will be your God" (Jer 11:2, 4). But his message is that Jerusalem had violated the covenant and so would be punished by YHWH through destruction and deportation (see Jer 22:8-9). The notion of *punishment for broken covenant* dominates the first half of the book of Jeremiah. Consequently the prophet anticipated divine punishment enacted through Babylonian servitude (28:14). By 29:3-9, the prophet writes the deportees to tell them to accept the exile as their God-given destiny. Thus the prophet completes the first part of his calling, the work of "plucking up and tearing down, destroying and overthrowing" (1:10).

The remarkable thing about the book of Jeremiah, however, is that the destruction and deportation are not the final word of God to Israel. Thus the prophet takes up the second part of his vocational mandate, "to plant and to build" (Jer 1:10). His work is to voice and construct a livable future for Israel that God wills. The prophet, grounded in God's faithfulness, dares to imagine that out of the abyss of exilic abandonment God will yet be faithful and will yet do good for Israel. The articulation of this remarkable hope is given in chapters 29-33 where the book clusters oracles and narratives of divine promise. More specifically, Jer 30:2 speaks of "a book" (scroll) that many interpreters believe was an independent collection

IV. The Landscape of Jeremiah's Sojourn

of oracles of hope in chapters 30–31 that was subsequently incorporated into the larger scroll. These two chapters are called "The Book of Comfort" or "The Book of Consolation." These oracles assure that Israel has a future because God loves Israel and remains true to Israel, even in its season of exile and abandonment. A student of these oracles will do well to read out loud all of chapters 30–31. One may notice two matters in particular. First, in 30:22 (repeated from 11:4) is the so-called "covenant formula" reflecting the intimacy of the covenantal relationship:

> And you shall be my people,
> and I will be your God. (Jer 30:22)

It is as though the exile has not disrupted the relationship. Or better, that God has, in the season of abandonment, reenacted the relationship. Second, in 30:17, the poet uses a technical formula, "restore the fortunes," to indicate that God will reverse the future of Israel from evil to good (see Jer 29:14; 32:44; 33:11, 26).

In the midst of these several promissory oracles, the best known (and perhaps most important) is the announcement of "new covenant" in Jer 31:31–34. This oracle declares that the old covenant of Sinai has been broken by the waywardness of Israel, not unlike the breaking of the covenant in Exod 32. But now, in the depth of the abyss, God resolves to renew, restore, or reenact the covenant. Thus it is "new," but in the sense of being "renewed." God wills and is resolved to have a relationship of fidelity with Israel, even though Israel has evidenced profound fickleness in the past. That new covenant, like the old, includes the commandments of Torah ("my law"); only now there will be glad willingness on the part of Israel to obey the Torah commandments (in contrast to the old recalcitrance). As a consequence the oracle reiterates yet again the covenant formula, "I will be their God and they shall be my people." The oracle anticipates an open, free, trusting, responsive relationship in time to come. And that new relationship is grounded in nothing other than God's readiness to "forgive and forget." What has happened in the past that brought divine punishment (and that preoccupied Jeremiah for so long) no longer pertains. God is willing to start afresh and anticipates a like readiness on the part of Israel. The future depends upon God's forgiveness!

We may reflect in two ways on the "new covenant." First, it is clear that the "new covenant" pertains to Israel. It is a long-standing mistake in the church to think that the new covenant is with reference to Jesus. It is not!

But second, the quotation of this passage in Heb 8:8–12 makes clear that some in the early church affirmed that Jesus is "the mediator of a better covenant" (Heb 8:6). Thus the oracle is seen to spill over into Christian claims. There is a great temptation (that must be resisted) to preempt the oracle for Christian faith, but that is to misuse the oracle of the prophet.

Thus the future of Judaism, in this text, depends upon God's readiness for renewed covenant. This motif is extended in subsequent prophetic utterance. In a retrospect on the land (field) of Jeremiah, the covenant formula is repeated in 32:38 where the covenant is characterized as "eternal," that is, beyond abrogation:

> I will make an everlasting covenant with them, never to draw back from doing good to them; and I will put the fear of me in their hearts, so that they may not turn from me. I will rejoice in doing good to them, and I will plant them in this land in faithfulness, with all my heart and all my soul. (Jer 32:40–41)

And in 33:20–21, 25, the covenant with David, with the Levites, with Jacob, with the offspring of Abraham, Isaac, and Jacob—that is, with Israel—is as reliable as the covenant the creator has with day and night, with "the ordinances of heaven and earth":

> If any of you could break my covenant with the day and my covenant with the night, so that day and night would not come at their appointed time, only then could my covenant with my servant David be broken, so that he would not have a son to reign on his throne and my covenant with my ministers, the Levites ... Only if I had not established my covenant with day and night, and the ordinances of heaven and earth, would I reject the offspring of Jacob and of my servant David and not choose any of his descendants as rulers over the offspring of Abraham, Isaac, and Jacob. (Jer 33:20–21, 25–26).

The oracles of Jeremiah are the ground for immense hope in Israel. In his ministry of divine judgment ("pluck up and tear down"), Jeremiah had to overcome the *deep denial* of Jerusalem; now in his ministry of divine hope ("plant and build"), he has to overcome the *acute despair* of the exiles. The future of Israel, like the future of the world, depends upon God's profound fidelity that is enacted in forgiveness and passionate commitment. This is a passion for Israel that is not unlike the passion for a well-beloved child (Jer 31:20).

IV. The Landscape of Jeremiah's Sojourn

QUESTIONS FOR DISCUSSION

1. How do you imagine God as a covenant maker?
2. What does forgiveness cost the one who forgives?
3. How could it be that new possibility is available precisely in the depth of despair?
4. What covenants can you identify that have been broken and renewed?
5. How might you think differently about the Eucharist as "the cup of the new covenant" (1 Cor 12:25)?
6. What do Jews and Christians share about the covenant with God?

19

The River

Jeremiah 51:59-64

THE FINGERPRINT OF BABYLON is all over the book of Jeremiah. In the time of Jeremiah, Babylon was the principle superpower that constituted an endless threat to a series of small states, including Judah. Under Nebuchadnezzar, the expansionism of the Babylonian empire was aggressive; his army came three times into Judah. While that aggression against a small state is readily explained as characteristic expansionism, the book of Jeremiah thought otherwise about the empire. It insisted that Nebuchadnezzar was in fact an agent of YHWH, so that the Babylonian incursions into Jerusalem constituted divine punishment for covenantal violation. In that bold interpretive stance, Nebuchadnezzar is identified as a "servant of YHWH":

> I am going to send for all the tribes of the north, says the LORD, even for King Nebuchadnezzar of Babylon, *my servant* . . . (Jer 25:9)

> Now I have given all these lands into the hand of King Nebuchadnezzar of Babylon, *my servant,* and I have given him even the wild animals from the field to serve him. (Jer 27:6)

YHWH is allied with Babylon at the expense of Jerusalem.

This alliance is of God and Babylon was an acute vexation to Israel. The great promises of YHWH in Jer 30–31 clearly imagined a future for Jerusalem beyond Babylonian displacement. These promises, however,

IV. The Landscape of Jeremiah's Sojourn

were surely blocked by the geo-political reality of Babylon whose policies prevented homecoming for Israel.

It is for that reason that the book of Jeremiah includes, as do many of the prophetic books, a collection of Oracles Against the Nations (see also Isa 13–23; Ezek 25–32; and Amos 1–2). The oracles, in a highly stylized way, accuse the nations of arrogant autonomy who eventually must submit to the sovereignty of YHWH. Thus even the great states, the superpowers, cannot circumvent the rule of YHWH.

In the book of Jeremiah these oracles are presented in chapters 46–51. They are arranged so that they begin with the second superpower, Egypt (46) and culminate with Babylon (50–51). In between, a number of lesser states are also called to account (47–49). Our interest, however, is in the oracle concerning Babylon. The oracle begins with a stunning announcement about the ultimate defeat of Babylon and the humiliation of the Babylonian gods:

> Declare among the nations and proclaim,
> > set up a banner and proclaim,
> > do not conceal it, say:
> *Babylon is taken,*
> > Bel is put to shame,
> > Merodach is dismayed.
> Her images are put to shame,
> > her idols are dismayed. (Jer 50:2)

When one reads on, it is clear that YHW has dispatched human agents (in this case, Cyrus the Persian; Jer 50:8–10, 18, 31–32; 51:1–5). It turns out that YHWH's utilization of Babylon was quite provisional in the long run. YHWH will not stay linked to any nation-state or to any superpower. YHWH has now become an adversary of Babylon and is intent on the homecoming of Israel to which Babylon would never assent.

The concluding paragraph of 51:59–64 gives dramatic expression to the termination of Babylon in a way that entails emancipation for Israel. The prophet dispatches a scribe (a scroll-man), Seraiah, to produce a scroll on which is written the content of chapters 50–51. The words of course are a threat against the empire. After the reading, Seraiah is to throw the scroll into the Euphrates River (the great river of Babylon) accompanied by these words: "Thus shall Babylon sink, to rise no more, because of the disasters that I am bringing on her" (51:64). The *sinking of the scroll* into the river signifies the *sinking of Babylon* into non-being. The act is not more than street-theatre, but the act invites a perception of Babylon as subject to the terminating intention of YHWH. We read the text and are permitted to imagine the sinking of the empire as well. The concluding formula of v. 64 suggests that this is the end of the words of Jeremiah. Nothing more needs to be said. Nothing more can be said. Superpowers may posture and threaten, and prevail for a time. In the end, however, superpowers are flimsy arrangements of power that cannot stand in the face of YHWH's intention.

This dramatic act by the scribe is rightly matched to historical reality. Soon after the death of Nebuchadnezzar (962 BCE), Cyrus the Persian came from the east as a "bird of prey" to defeat Babylon (see Isa 46:11). How strange that this Babylonian empire, so powerful and seemingly beyond challenge, abruptly vanished from history!

The dramatic action of the scribe—and the ensuing historical eventuality—accomplished two things. First, it asserted the ultimate rule of God in the face of every pretension. The liturgy of Jerusalem had long asserted YHWH's rule over the nations:

> Say among the nations, "The LORD is king!" (Ps 96:10)

And indeed, the ultimate affirmation of the Book of Revelation imagines all nations eventually being subject to the rule of God:

> The kingdom of the world has become the kingdom of our Lord
> And of his Messiah,
> And he will reign forever and ever. (Rev 11:15)

But second, the defeat of Babylon means that Israel is freed for homecoming, for the end of exile, and restoration to well-being. This affirmation is given right in the middle of the denunciation of Babylon:

> I will restore Israel to its pasture, and it shall feed on Carmel and in Bashan, and on the hills of Ephraim, and in Gilead its hunger shall be satisfied. In those days and at that time, says the LORD, the iniquity of Israel shall be sought, and there shall be none; and the sins of Judah, and none shall be found; for I will pardon the remnant that I have spared. (Jer 50:19–20)

It is now possible that the great divine promises of chapters 30–31 can be implemented:

> See, I am going to bring them from the land of the north,
>   and gather them from the farthest parts of the earth,

> among them the blind and the lame,
>> those with child and those in labor, together;
>> a great company, they shall return here.
> With weeping they shall come,
>> and with consolation I will lead them back,
> I will let them walk by brooks of water,
>> in a straight path in which they shall not stumble;
> for I have become a father to Israel,
>> and Ephraim is my firstborn . . .
> For the Lord has ransomed Jacob,
>> and has redeemed him from hands too strong for him.
> They shall come and sing aloud on the height of Zion,
>> and they shall be radiant over the goodness of the Lord,
> over the grain, the wine, and the oil,
>> and over the young of the flock and the herd;
> their life shall become like a watered garden,
>> and they shall never languish again (Jer 31:8–9, 11–12)

It is as though the destruction and deportation were at best a blip on the screen of memory. That wounding episode did indeed leave a deep scar on Israel's relationships with YHWH. But it is not defining for the future of that relationship. What counts is the ultimate fidelity of God. The book of Jeremiah finishes with a glad homecoming. The savage judgment earlier enacted on Jerusalem is now reassigned to Babylon. In the end, the glory is to God the creator:

> It is he who made the earth by his power,
>> who established the world by his wisdom,
>> and by his understanding stretched out the heavens.
> When he utters his voice there is a tumult of waters in the heavens,
>> and he makes the mist rise from the ends of the earth.
> He makes lightnings for the rain,
>> and he brings out the wind from his storehouses.
> (Jer 51:15–16; see 10:12–13)

The news of that God is good for God's people!

> Not like these is the Lord, the portion of Jacob,
>> for he is the one who formed all things,
> and Israel is the tribe of his inheritance;
>> the Lord of hosts is his name.
> (Jer 51:19; see 10:16)

QUESTIONS FOR DISCUSSION

1. Can superpowers for a time block God's intention?
2. Do you think superpowers ever learn anything about being penultimate?
3. Do you think we in the United States can read this text and understand what it is like to be a little state in the face of the empire?
4. Do you think the disappearance of Babylon from world history has a counterpoint in the disappearance of the Soviet Union from world history? Do you think there are other superpowers among us who might also disappear from world history?
5. In what ways might the United States as a superpower be engaged in this text?
6. What would you throw into the river if you had a chance to go to the Euphrates?

20

Back to Basics

The abrupt turn of our national political economy toward uncritical populism (with a tilt toward fascism) has bewildered many preachers including this one. That turn has made preaching for many of us even more difficult and demanding, because ideological sensibilities are so acute, and every utterance seems freighted with risk. That turn, however, has also made preaching more urgent, because it signifies that we are in a time of forgetfulness, or what Michael Fishbane has called "mindlessness."[1] It is as though in raw and ready ideological dispute we have forgotten the glue of the national good. And a spin-off of that forgetfulness means that we have to some extent in the church forgotten the ties that bind us in the gospel to the living God and to each other.

I.

In such a season of forgetfulness (mindlessness), I suggest that we preachers must go back to the basics of what we must remember that we have forgotten. Or in Fishbane's parlance, we must be intentionally "mindful" in a context of pathological mindlessness. When we go back to basics, I propose that we may (without being excessively didactic) bear witness to the ethical completion of the good news or in Bonhoeffer's language, that we may exposit the "cost of discipleship." My impression is that with a generous accent on God's good grace, we are in sum very close to "cheap grace"

1. Fishbane, *Sacred Attunement*.

in order to reassure and comfort in a way that requires no costly or even inconvenient decision. The ethical completion of the gospel tradition is everywhere evident. It is voiced at Sinai in response to the Decalogue: "All that the LORD has spoken we will do and we will be obedient" (Exod 24:7).

In Jesus' ministry it is "follow me" that means to cease to follow the path of Rome:

> Jesus calls us o'er the tumult for life's restless sea;
> day by day his sweet voice soundeth saying, "Christian follow me."[2]

In Paul's language, it is to be "of the same mind" that means to "look to the interest of others" (Phil 2:4–5), that our minds may be renewed and transformed with what is good and acceptable and perfect (Rom 12:2). Cultural Christianity among us comes packaged as a reassurance that there is no compelling "ask" in the gospel, or the "ask" among right-wing Christians is simply an echo of dominant cultural values. In truth, however, the gospel is a summons to be different, think differently, imagine differently, save, spend, and invest differently, and act differently. I recognize that in exploring the "cost" of discipleship it is futile in most venues to focus on current hot-button issues; better in my judgment go back to basics that lie behind such issues.

The "basics" concerning "cost" are most succinctly put in the two "great commandments" (Matt 22:34–40; Mark 12:28–34; Luke 10:25–28). In Mark they asked Jesus for the first commandment; he answered, "You cannot have one; you get two." You cannot separate God and human reality. In response to Jesus the scribe conceded that all the punctilious requirements of piety count for nothing in the face of the two commandments. In Luke the lawyer knows the answer, and Jesus promises him that the two commandments will bring life; the negative implication, I take it, is that neglect of these two commandments will inescapably bring a death. In Matthew, Jesus concludes his response by affirming: "On these two commandments hang all the law and the prophets" (Matt 22:40). The "law and prophets" refers to the Torah of Moses (law) and the prophetic corpus, that is, in sum the "canonical" tradition of Judaism. To say it all "hangs" on these two commandments evokes the interpretive verdict of Paul who, it turns out, is not so fixed on grace that he cannot notice the commandments:

> For the whole law [Torah] is summed up in a single commandment, "You shall love your neighbor as yourself . . . Bear one

2. Alexander, "Jesus Call Us," in *Glory to God*, 720.

another's burdens, and in this way you will fulfill the law of Christ. (Gal 5:14; see 6:2)

Paul seems indeed to reduce the two great commandments to one, but for Paul the first is surely implied and assumed in the second. Thus I propose that a preacher who seeks to be a pedagogue about the "cost" might spend energy expositing the two great commandments that together constitute the mark of difference for those who have been called to discipleship. Such an exposition can avoid simplistic reductions and over time can fully articulate the riskiness of an alternative life in gospel faith. Over time this would also entail a recovery of baptism as a serious world-changing sacrament.[3]

II.

The first great commandment, love of God, is quoted in the gospel from Deut 6:5. This gives the preacher an opportunity to help the congregation rediscover (or discover for the first time) the book of Deuteronomy. It may also be that the preacher will discover Deuteronomy for the first time. Clearly for almost all church people the book of Deuteronomy is part of an undifferentiated mass of old stuff easily dismissed. But "back to basics" surely requires that the preacher must spend time in the book of Deuteronomy, because that book is the dynamic center of covenantal theology that was actively on the horizon of Jesus and the early church.

A beginning point is to discern the dynamic tradition that the book of Deuteronomy practices and embodies. The book is clearly rooted in the old Mosaic memory and so is presented as the teaching of Moses. The work of Moses in this belated text is to rearticulate the covenant for a new time, place, and circumstance, namely, life in the land of promise. Thus at the outset Moses is said to "expound" this Torah (Deut 1:5). That is, Moses exposited the old memory of Sinai and by expounding he gave fresh articulation and extended the rule of God into spheres of life that were not in purview at Sinai.

In Deut 5:3, moreover, Moses declares: "Not with our ancestors did the LORD make this covenant, but with us, who are all of us here alive today." Moses indicates that the dynamism of the covenant requires on-going

---

3. Attention should be paid to the forthcoming book of Alan Streett, *Caesar and the Sacrament: Baptism A Rite of Resistance*. Streett proposes that in quite explicit ways baptism in the early church imitated imperial practice and served as an alternative to the imperial rite that it imitated.

imaginative interpretation that precludes any package of fundamentalism or the certitudes of "originalism." The book of Deuteronomy is exactly such imaginative interpretation that transposes the covenant for a context of royal power and a predatory political economy, perhaps in the eighth century BCE.

The core mandate of the covenant is exactly "love of God": "You shall love the LORD your God with all your heart, and with all your soul, and with all your might" (Deut 6:5). But then Moses, in Deuteronomy, proceeds to show at great length that "love" means obedience to the commandments (12–25). This extended corpus of commands discloses the character and will of the God whom we are to love fully, without reservation, by our intentional, disciplined acts. That is, love is a *praxis*, action informed by the normative narrative of covenant to which we have sworn allegiance.

Our "love of God" reflects, is responsive to, and corresponds to the character of this God who is disclosed here, and we say more fully in Jesus of Nazareth. For starters we may identify three marks of this covenantal God that are to inform our obedience:

1. The God of covenant is a *forgiving* God who "restores the fortunes" after God's people have been wayward and recalcitrant (Deut 30:3; for use of the same phrase see Jer 29:14; 30:3; 33:7, 11, 26). In response, God's people are to be a forgiving people. This is evident in what is the core command of Deuteronomy, "the year of releases" in Deut 15:1–18. It is provided that debts should be cancelled, most particularly on poor people, every seven years. This commandment shows that "forgiveness" is elementally an economic process that concerns the forgiveness of debts. Thus in one version of the Lord's Prayer we pray that our debts may be forgiven. God does not want anyone to be permanently in hock. God does not want there to be a permanent underclass in hopeless debt; God intends that our economy should be subordinated to and in the service of covenantal neighborliness.

This mandate of forgiveness is voiced (then and now) in a debt-propelled economy in which the "haves" depend upon the cheap labor of the "have-nots" and keep the "have-nots" permanently in debt so that they can be devoured by interest rates (see Deut 23:19–20). It is clear that Moses encountered resistance to this radical act forgiveness, for he declares that God's people should not be "hard-hearted or tight-fisted" when it comes to forgiveness of debts (15:7). The antithesis of forgiveness is *bookkeeping* or score-keeping in which careful records are kept (at least in memory) so that we know who owes whom, who has offended whom, and who must "make payment," whether monetary or relational.[4] This bookkeeping mentality allows no slippage for human need or vulnerability, but requires full unadjusted paying up. Thus the poor must "earn food stamps," immigrants must "qualify," and those who default end with eviction, deportation, or imprisonment.[5] Covenant people are to act differently as an act of love of God, not only in face-to-face dealings, but in policy formation so that a forgiving community and a debt-cancelling economy are acts of "love of God."

2. The God of covenant is *a God of hospitality* who welcomes into the community and into the political economy those who are inconvenient. This is the God who

> Executes justice for the orphan and the widow, and who loves the strangers, providing them food and clothing. (Deut 10:18)

Imagine God making provision for food and clothing for those outside "the tribe"! That provision, moreover, is said to be an "execution of justice," so that the needs of orphan, widow, and immigrant are not charity but a just right. From this it promptly follows that the covenant people is to act as YHWH acts:

> You shall love the stranger, for you were strangers in the land of Egypt (10:19).

The faithful are to replicate the hospitable action of God. As a result, the commandments of Deuteronomy are preoccupied with practical hospitality toward the vulnerable (the poor, widow, orphan, immigrant) who by their presence are "entitled" to economic viability (Deut 24:10–15, 17–22). The resources of the community are to be distributed not on the basis of power, but on the basis of presence and need.

This act of mandated hospitality toward the vulnerable is contrasted with the condescension of "charity."[6] Charity, that so many people and so many congregations embrace, is not a serious recognition of the legitimate claims of the needy, but only a gesture of patronage by the "haves" out of their surplus that can be done without cost or much inconvenience. Moses clearly has in mind covenantal hospitality that is committed to justice and not to condescending patronage. Thus the commandments make provision

---

4. I am grateful to Peter Block who suggested to me the term "bookkeeping" as an antithesis to forgiveness.

5. See Desmond, *Evicted: Poverty and Profit in the American City*.

6. I am grateful to John McKnight who suggested to me the term "charity" as an antithesis to hospitality.

for the protection and performance of the "right" of the vulnerable that goes well beyond charity.

3. The God of covenant is a *God of generosity:*

> The LORD your God will make you abundantly prosperous in all your undertakings, in the fruit of your body, in the fruit of your livestock, and in the fruit of your soil. For the LORD will again take delight in prospering you . . . (Deut 30:9)

The sermonic rhetoric of Moses functions to remind the covenant people that all that they have is a gift of God's goodness:

> When the LORD your God has brought you into the land that he swore to your ancestors, to Abraham, to Isaac, and to Jacob, to give you—a land with fine, large cities that you did not build, houses filled with all sorts of goods that you did not fill, hewn cisterns that you did not hew, vineyards and olive groves that you did not plant . . . (Deut 6:10–11)

> When you have eaten your fill and have built fine houses and live in them, and when your herds and flocks have multiplied, and your silver and gold is multiplied, and all that you have is multiplied . . . Do not say to yourself, "My power and the might of my own hand have gotten me this wealth." But remember the LORD your God, for it is he who gives you power to get wealth . . . (Deut 8:12–13, 17–18)

Imagining that one is self-made and self-sufficient can lead to cynical parsimony: The money mine; I don't owe anything to anyone." The propensity in our predatory economy to deny generosity toward the vulnerable is a function of the illusion self-sufficiency in which the awareness of the "neighbor" disappears from consciousness. We then enjoy a torrent of self-congratulatory, self-preoccupied greed that regards the needy neighbor as a threat, not entitled to any generosity. The impetus for generosity, in the rhetoric of Moses, is found in the awareness that God is the creator who gives all good gifts. ("We give thee but thine own.") These gifts are to be shared generously as the creator has been generous.

The tradition of Deuteronomy incessantly warns about "other gods" who are precluded by the first commandment of Sinai, "No other gods" (Exod 20:3–6; Deut 5:6–10). In Deuteronomy the "other gods" are ciphers for all that oppose the covenant God of forgiveness, hospitality, and generosity. The cipher "Canaanite" signifies a social practice that reduces all relations to monetary transactions and reduces all neighbors to commodities.

Thus the "religion of Baal" comes with the socio-economic practices of *bookkeeping* (not forgiveness), *charity* (not hospitality), and *parsimony* (not generosity). The religious symbols of Baal are to be destroyed because they are icons of the commoditization of human relationships and thus the denial of neighborly attentiveness (Deut 7:5).

It requires no imagination at all to see that our own contemporary monetization of social relationships (concerning health care, tax policy, bank deregulation) serve to enhance the powerful with endless expansion of economic resources at the expense of the vulnerable who are without resources. Such monetization of social reality permits and authorizes the endless predatory exploitation of the vulnerable other. In the midst of that economy where we now live, to "love God" is a mighty alternative to the idols, an act that intends to interrupt such practice and policy.

> Jesus calls us from the worship of the vain world's golden store,
> from each idol that would keep us, saying, *Christian, love me more."*
> In our joys and in our sorrows, days of toil and hours of ease,
> still he calls, in cares and pleasures, *"Christian, love me more than these."*

Thus the Torah of Deuteronomy, a first guideline on how to "love God," is a "glimpse of a new order that is the kingdom of God."[7] The "kingdom of God" is not a never-never land of "life after death" as we so easily conclude when we reduce faith to "spiritual" matters to the neglect of the material. It is rather an alternative practice of social relationships that correspond to the social practices of the covenantal God. I propose that a "back to the basics" invites the preacher to exposit "love of God." It is unnecessary and unhelpful for the preacher to take sides or speak about the great theoretical codes of capitalism, socialism, etc., for those dogmas constitute a distraction from the first great commandment to love God without reservation. There is more to be said about the first great commandment than is offered in the book of Deuteronomy. That book, nevertheless, is a poignant place from which to begin. Since the scroll remains unopened in much of the church, this may be a fresh pedagogical moment in which the preacher can replicate Ezra: "So they read from the book, from the Torah of God, with interpretation. They gave sense, so that the people understood the reading" (Neh 8:8).

---

7. Miller, *Israelite Religion and Biblical Theology*, 502.

III.

The second great commandment, love of neighbor, is quoted in the gospels from Lev 19.[8] This gives the preacher a chance to help the congregation rediscover) or discover for the first time) the book of Leviticus. It may also be that the preacher will discover it for the first time. Clearly for almost all church people the book of Leviticus is part of an undifferentiated an disregarded mass of old stuff readily dismissed. The only exception is that we may pick out a few preferred verses from the book, as for example Lev 18 with which to flail gays. But "back to basics" surely means that the preacher must spend time in the book of Leviticus because it is a launching pad for an ongoing disputatious reflection on the holiness of God's people, a question that was actively on the horizon of Jesus. Thus his dispute in Mark 7:1–23 on "what goes in" and "what comes out" as defiling is all about holiness. When we recite the creed, moreover, we affirm the "one *holy*, catholic and apostolic church," surely without excessive reflection on holiness.

The teaching point for the preacher is that God's people (all of the baptized community) are called to holiness that corresponds to the holiness of God: "You shall be holy for I the LORD your God am holy" (Lev 19:2). The verses that immediately follow allude to the commandment on honoring mother and father, keeping Sabbath, and refusing idols and images (vv. 3–4).We may assume that the remainder of the Decalogue is also implied in the statement, so that "holiness" comes to mean keeping Torah.

The book of Leviticus constitutes a long reflection on the form holiness may take for the people of God; clearly the book reflects an ongoing dispute among the priests about the nature of holiness, a discussion and dispute that continues among us. I suggest that one important question about holiness concerns one's posture toward "the other." There is ample evidence in the book of Leviticus that holiness requires careful avoidance of the *other* because the other will defile and contaminate. Thus holiness runs in the direction of cleanness and purity.[9] As is readily recognized, Lev 19 is peculiarly and strategically positioned between chapters 18 and 20 that are preoccupied with prohibited "distorted" sexual relationships. And even in chapter 19 we get worry about possible dangerous "mixing": "You shall not let your animals breed with a different kind; you shall not sow your field with two kinds of seed; nor shall you put on a garment made of two

---

8. Goodman, *Love Thy Neighbor as Thyself.*
9. See Beck, *Unclean.*

IV. The Landscape of Jeremiah's Sojourn

different materials" (v. 19).[10] From this fear of "mixing" it is an easy step to far of human "mixing." Thus later on, in the interest of maintaining a "holy tribe," Ezra is warned about the danger that "the holy seed (semen) has been mixed" (Ezra 9:2). Such a concern is surely an anticipation of modern fears about "mixed races." And while all of that seems old fashioned in an embarrassing way, Bill Bishop, in his book, *The Big Sort*, has chronicled the way in which "red" and "blue" people are self-selecting to like-minded communities of work, housing, and worship; conservatives and liberals currently want to live in communities of pure ideology . . . echoes of the holiness agenda of Ezra![11]

It is clear in Lev 19, however, there is a counter-point of holiness that purposes a very different way with "the other." I suggest that we might perceive in holiness tradition a continuing escalation and expansion of positive engagement with the other, an engagement that anticipates the judgment of Emmanuel Lévinas that the "face of the other" is where we meet the truth of our lives.[12]

1. The commandment of Lev 19:18, quoted in the gospels, alludes to *love of self* along with love of neighbor. There is no doubt that the covenantal tradition advocates a healthy self-respect, a self-respect that is reflected and voiced in the lament psalms that freely state before God the legitimate claims of the self.[13] Such a healthy sense of self that is indispensable for generative love of neighbor is very different from the narcissistic self-indulgence of so much of our selfie culture. Healthy self-regard as a component of holiness does not need always to advertise and exhibit the self. Such exhibits are not necessary when the self is healthy.

2. But of course the commandment of Lev 19:18 is occupied with the neighbor: *Love neighbor* as much as self! "Neighbor," in the tradition, means fellow members of the covenant community, all its members who are distinguished from "foreigners" who are not neighbors." But of course the tradition and most especially Jesus keeps the question open: "Who is my neighbor?" and continues to expand the zone of neighborliness. But

---

10. Mary Douglas, *Purity and Danger: An Analysis of Concepts of Pollution and Taboo*, has established a major thesis that impurity and profanation in the old holiness codes was constituted by having things out of place, in the wrong place, or mixed with other things inappropriately.

11. Bishop, *The Big Sort: Why the Clustering of Like-Minded America Is Tearing Us Apart*.

12. Lévinas, *Totality and Infinity: An Essay on Exteriority*.

13. See Wolterstorff, *Justice in Love*, 94–97, on "Is Self-love Legitimate?"

even before that zone is greatly expanded, this trajectory of interpretation envisions a neighborhood for the common good in which the self is not free to keep from the neighborhood what is required for viability. Thus: "With justice you shall judge your neighbor" (v. 15). Holiness is characterized as justice for the neighbor, a practice that assures viable sustenance for all the neighbors! The same accent, moreover, is clear in the tenth commandment that sounds the word "neighbor" three times in its prohibition of acquisitiveness:

> You shall not covet your *neighbor's* house; you shall not covet your *neighbor's* wife, or male or female slave or ox or donkey, or anything that belongs to your *neighbor*. (Exod 20:17)

And in our much cited v. 18, love of neighbor is a counter to vengeance or grudge, thus affirming the legitimacy of the neighbor. It is, moreover, remarkable that this accent on neighbor is situated exactly in the holiness tradition. Thus engagement with the neighbor is a way to "take time to be holy." This teaching surely witnesses against the holiness trajectory of purity and cleanness that accents disengagement from the neighbor who may contaminate.

3. This vision of love of neighbor is pushed further in our chapter with attentiveness to the *poor neighbor*:

> You shall not strip your vineyard bare, or gather the fallen grapes of your vineyard; you shall leave them for the poor and the alien: I am the LORD your God. (Lev 19:10)

The poor have a special claim on the community that has obligation to provide an adequate safety net that precludes all "laws of enclosure." Indeed care for the poor is seen in the tradition to be an equivalent to knowledge of God:

> He [the king] judged the cause of the poor and needy;
> Then it was well.
> Is this not to know me" says the LORD. (Jer 22:16)

The wisdom tradition, moreover, sees the special linkage of the poor to God:

> Those who oppress the poor insult their Maker;
> but those who are kind to the needy honor him. (Prov 14:11)

It is an easy step from here to the instruction of Jesus that

IV. The Landscape of Jeremiah's Sojourn

> Just as you did it to one of the least of thee who are members of my family, you did it to me. (Matt 25:40)

4. While the "poor" are noticed and supported by the community, the text reaches further toward "the other" with reference to *the immigrant (alien)*.[14] The immigrant is named along with the poor in v. 10. But more important is this:

> The alien who resides with you shall be to you as a citizen among you; you shall love the alien as yourself, for you were aliens in the land of Egypt: I am the LORD your God. (Lev 19:34)

The phrasing is exactly the same as in v. 18: "neighbor as yourself," "immigrant as yourself"!

Verse 34 is quite remarkable. Holiness means embrace of the other who is not a member of "our tribe." Though the holiness tradition of Leviticus does not go further, we notice in Deuteronomy that along with the immigrant come *the widow and orphan*, so that we may take this triad of the vulnerable as the ultimate agenda of holiness. Holiness has to do, in this trajectory, with restorative practices toward the vulnerable who have been diminished by the hard-hearted, tight-fisted practices of predation.

5. To be sure this tradition in the Hebrew Bible does not go as far as "love your *enemy*," an extension of Torah that was voiced by Jesus.

> But I say to you, Love your enemies and pray for those who persecute you, so that you may be children of your Father in heaven. (Matt 5:44)

It is worth noting that this paragraph of instruction by Jesus ends in this way: "Be perfect, therefore, as your heavenly father is perfect" (v. 48). This is a quote from Lev 19:2. Jesus links *love of enemy* to *the imperative to be holy!* Thus we may see that this mapping of the other imagines an always extended, always expanding zone of neighborliness that constitutes holiness: self ... neighbor ... poor ... immigrant (widow and orphan) ... enemy! In his assault on the punctilious piety of the "scribes and Pharisees," moreover, Jesus attests that the weightier matters of the Torah (that is, the practice of holiness) consist not in scrupulous tithing but in "justice, mercy, and faith" (Matt 2:23-24). Jesus continues to up-end the holiness tradition, an impulse already activated in Lev 19.

---

14. On the "stranger," see Spina, "Israelites as Gerim."

The preacher may reflect on the "task of othering" that belongs to holiness, and may acknowledge the vigorous contestation in which folks (all of us!) are engaged: the other as neighbor or the other as threat. I commend *The Clash Within* in which Martha Nussbaum considers the way in which each of us hosts a "clash within" concerning the *welcome* of the other and *fear* of the other.[15] That "clash," suggests Nussbaum, is inescapable. What matters is how we manage it; it will be managed in more healthy ways when it is named and processed in honest ways. The matter of the *other* remains unsettled for each of us' for that reason the issue compels attention from the preacher. The covenantal tradition, even in Leviticus, has a dynamic notion of "othering" and there is no more urgent issue now before our society with its propensity to exclusionary fear and tribal anxiety. There is more to be said about "love of neighbor" than Lev 19. But this is a teachable place in which to begin.

IV.

"Back to basics" means, I suggest, articulating and processing the profound either /or of our baptisms, an either/or as old as Moses, as urgent as Jesus, and as contemporary among us as the recognition of our monetized political economy. I have found most helpful the either/or of Paul's articulation of "the desires of the flesh" and "the fruit of the spirit." I am deeply informed by the discussion of Brigitte Kahl who understands Paul's discussion of "the law" in Galatians as a challenge to the Roman Empire (and even, I extrapolate, as a challenge to the US "law of money and sex.")[16] That is, the "law" that preoccupies Paul is not the Torah of Judaism but the rule and expectation of the empire. The empire of Rome had its requirements and expectations for making it big in the empire; the requirement was readiness to participate in a predatory political economy. That dominant value system, everywhere imposed, specialized in "the desires of the flesh" that consisted in mean-spirited self-promotion and uncaring self-indulgence. The empire functioned to generate appetites that could be satisfied only by anti-neighborly action. Paul offers an inventory of behaviors that arise from the embrace of such appetites:

---

15. Nussbaum, *The Clash Within*.
16. Kahl, *Galatians Re-Imagined*.

IV. The Landscape of Jeremiah's Sojourn

> Now the works of the flesh are obvious: fornication, impurity, licentiousness, idolatry, sorcery, enmities, strife, jealousy, anger, quarrels, dissensions, factions, envy, drunkenness, and carousing, and things like these. (Gal 5:19–21)

It will require some careful pedagogy to let people see that "the desires of the flesh" are not simply drugs, alcohol, and sex, but are practices of anti-neighborliness that put the satiation of the self at the center of reality. Paul's awareness is that one cannot subscribe to the values of the predatory economy of sex and money and not have these social outcomes.

The baptismal alternative is to refuse participation in that dominant value system (a refusal enacted by Daniel in Dan 1) in order to practice an alternative of covenantal neighborliness toward the neighbor, the poor, the immigrant, and the enemy. Neighborliness requires a refusal of the militarized consumerism that is justified by US exceptionalism, even as Rome knew itself to be "exceptional."[17] Opting for neighborliness (love of neighbor) yields the fruit of the spirit:

> The fruit of the Spirit is love, joy, peace, patience, kindness, generosity, faithfulness, gentleness, and self-control. There is no law against such things. (Gal 5:22–23)

As Paul knew, one cannot have that "fruit" while participating in the dominant "law" of the empire.

It is the work of the preacher to connect the dots. Our participation in the dominant system is so "normal" that we do not notice. As a result our life is caught up in endless TV ads, mostly concerning new care and more drugs that will kill us. It is assumed among us that more consumer goods will make us happy. It is assumed that more aggressive militarism will make us safe. It is assumed that more soccer practices will make us more ready for college applications. It is assumed that more spectator sports will give us companionship. It is assumed that anger toward Muslims is appropriate and can be unrestrained. All of these assumptions are sponsored by the empire and are regarded as "normal." It is assumed that it is OK to treat the other as a commodity or as an object without merit who qualifies for no respect, compassion, or justice. It is remarkable that Paul frames his

---

17. Paarlberg, *The United States of Excess: Gluttony and the Dark Side of American Exceptionalism*, has shown the way in which US Exceptionalism lies behind the national epidemic of obesity.

catalogues of "desires of the flesh" and "fruit of the spirit" by these two remarkable neighbor assertions that I have cited above:

> For the whole Torah is summed up in a single commandment: "You shall love your neighbor as yourself . . . Bear one another's burdens, and in this way you will fulfill the law of Christ. (Gal 5:14; see 6:2)

Kahl concludes:

> Apart from the works of imperial law, these faith works of love for Paul are indispensable, an insight that has been obscured by the abstract Protestant antithesis of faith versus works. Love of neighbor as yourself as the complete fulfillment of Torah (5:14) and the "new" law of Christ (5:6; 6:2) does not abandon Jewish law as such but rather the competitive and combative hierarchy of self and other that is at the core of Roman imperial *nomos*.[18]

It is the *nomos* of the US empire that is on offer as alternative to the two great commandments. That alternative, as we are now seeing so unmistakably, is lethal and makes a functioning humane community impossible.

This is a "back to basics" and on three counts. First, these slices of tradition and these elemental texts (Deuteronomy, Leviticus) are not known or available in the church, surely not in the lectionary. Second, the dots are not connected in the dominant narrative of the empire, and the empire has a great stake in making sure that they remain unconnected. Third, the two great commandments, with their enormous public implications, are themselves pre-political. They are in themselves accessible and without immense grand theory or ideology. They are "on the ground" elemental spin-offs of affirming that we are "sealed as Christ's own forever."

The task of the preacher, I propose, is to connect us to these old mandates of the tradition and to connect the dots from there to contemporary social reality and to the contemporary attitudes, actions, and policies that arise from these connections. To do this urgent pedagogy, I think, will require preachers to do textual study in more attentive ways, and to read more widely concerning "the empire of force" that so compels us.[19] I am aware that preachers do not have time for all of this. I wonder if the urgency of our context where God has put us requires an intentional shifting of priorities for the preacher to consider what the people of God now most

---

18. Kahl, *Galatians Re-Imagined*, 271–72.
19. See White, *Living Speech: Resisting the Empire of Force*.

require for living out our baptisms in faithful ways. "Back to basics" arises as an urgent task from the awareness that the truth entrusted to us contradicts the dominant narrative of imperial exceptionalism.

Bibliography

Adams, Samuel L. *Social and Economic Life in Second Temple Judea*. Louisville: Westminster John Knox, 2014.
Albertz, Rainer, and Rüdiger Schmitt. *Family and Household Religion in Ancient Israel and the Levant*. Winona Lake, IN: Eisenbrauns, 2012.
Alexander, Cecil Francis. "Jesus Calls Us." In *Glory to God: The Presbyterian Hymnal*, 720. Louisville: Westminster John Knox, 2013.
Anderson, Carol. *White Rage: The Unspoken Truth of Our Racial Divide*. New York: Bloomsbury, 2016.
Barth, Karl. *Church Dogmatics, III/2: The Doctrine of Creation Part Two*. Edited by G. W. Bromiley and T. F. Torrance. Translated by Harold Knight, et al. Edinburgh: T. & T. Clark, 1960.
———. *Church Dogmatics, IV/1: The Doctrine of Reconciliation, Part 1*. Edited by G. W. Bromiley and T. F. Torrance. Translated by G. W. Bromiley. Edinburgh: T. & T. Clark, 1956.
Beck, Richard. *Unclean: Meditations on Purity, Hospitality, and Morality*. Eugene, OR: Cascade Books, 2012.
Bishop, Bill. *The Big Sort: Why the Clustering of Like-Minded America Is Tearing Us Apart*. Boston: Mariner, 2009.
Book of Common Prayer. New York: Seabury, 1979.
"A Brief Statement of Faith." In *Glory to God: The Presbyterian Hymnal*, 38. Louisville: Westminster John Knox, 2013.
Brueggemann, Walter. *Solomon: Israel's Ironic Icon of Human Achievement*. Studies on Personalities of the Old Testament. Columbia: University of South Carolina, 2005.
Coates, Ta-Nehisi. *Between the World and Me*. New York: Random House, 2015.
Coffin, Henry Sloan. "The Book of Isaiah, Exposition." In *Interpreter's Bible*, vol. 5. Nashville: Abingdon, 1956.
Croly, George. "Spirit of God, Descend upon My Heart." In *Glory to God: The Presbyterian Hymnal*, 688. Louisville: Westminster John Knox Press, 2013.
Davis, Ellen F. *Biblical Prophecy: Perspectives for Christian Theology, Discipleship, and Ministry*. Interpretation. Louisville: Westminster John Knox, 2014.
Dear, John. "Back to Home." Jan. 16, 2007.
Dempsey, Carol J. *The Prophets: A Liberation-Critical Reading*. Liberation-Critical Reading of the Old Testament. Minneapolis: Fortress, 2000.
Desmond, Matthew. *Evicted: Poverty and Profit in the American City*. New York: Crown, 2016.

Bibliography

Douglas, Mary. *Purity and Danger: An Analysis of the Concept of Pollution and Taboo.* New York: Routledge, 2005.

Endo, Shusaku. *Silence: A Novel.* Translated by William Johnston. 1976. Reprint, New York: Picador, 2016.

Fishbane, Michael. *Sacred Attunement: A Jewish Theology.* Chicago: University of Chicago Press, 2008.

Fretheim, Terence E. *The Suffering of God: An Old Testament Perspective.* Overtures to Biblical Theology. Philadelphia: Fortress, 1984.

Gerstenberger, Erhard S. *Theologies in the Old Testament.* Translated by John Bowden. Minneapolis: Fortress, 2002.

Glory to God: The Presbyterian Hymnal. Louisville: Westminster John Knox, 2013.

Goodman, Lenn Evan. *Love Thy Neighbor as Thyself.* Oxford: Oxford University Press, 2008.

Janowski, Bernd. *Arguing with God: A Theological Anthropology of the Psalms.* Translated by Armin Siedlecki. Louisville: Westminster John Knox, 2013.

Kahl, Brigitte. *Galatians Re-Imagined: Reading with the Eyes of the Vanquished.* Paul in Critical Contexts. Minneapolis: Fortress, 2010.

Knohl, Israel. *The Sanctuary of Silence: The Priestly Torah and the Holiness School.* Winona Lake, IN: Eisenbrauns, 2007.

Lapsley, Jacqueline E. *Can These Bones Live? The Problem of the Moral Self in the Book of Ezekiel.* Beihefte zur Zeitschrift für die alttestamentliche Wissenschaft 301. Berlin: de Gruyter, 2000.

Lehmann, Paul. *The Transfiguration of Politics: The Presence and Power of Jesus of Nazareth in and over Human Affairs.* New York: Harper & Row, 1975.

Levenson, Jon D. *The Love of God: Divine Gift, Human Gratitude, and Mutual Faithfulness in Judaism.* Library of Jewish Ideas 8. Princeton: Princeton University Press, 2015.

Lévinas, Emmanuel. *Totality and Infinity: An Essay on Exteriority.* Pittsburgh: Duquesne University Press, 1969.

Lindström, Fredrik. *Suffering and Sin: Interpretations of Illness in the Individual Complaint Psalms.* Stockholm: Almqvist & Wiksell, 1994.

Macpherson, C. B. *The Political Theory of Possessive Individualism from Hobbes to Locke.* Oxford: Oxford University Press, 1962.

Miller, Patrick D. "The Human Sabbath: A Study in Deuteronomic Theology." *Princeton Seminary Bulletin* 6.2 (1985) 81–97.

———. *Israelite Religion and Biblical Theology: Collected Essays.* JSOTSup 267. Sheffield: Sheffield Academic, 2000.

———. *They Cried to the Lord: The Form and Theology of Biblical Prayer.* Minneapolis: Fortress, 1994.

Moltmann, Jürgen. *Theology of Hope: On the Ground and the Implications of a Christian Eschatology.* Translated by James W. Leitch. New York: Harper & Row, 1967.

Nussbaum, Martha. *The Clash Within: Democracy, Religious Violence, and India's Future.* Cambridge, MA: Belknap, 2008.

O'Brien, Julia M. *Challenging Prophetic Metaphor: Theology and Ideology in the Prophets.* Louisville: Westminster John Knox, 2008

O'Connor, Kathleen M. *Lamentations and the Tears of the World.* Maryknoll, NY: Orbis, 2002.

Paarlberg, Robert. *The United States of Excess: Gluttony and the Dark Side of American Exceptionalism.* Oxford: Oxford University Press, 2015.

Bibliography

Paton, Alan. "Meditation for a Young Boy Confirmed." *Christian Century*, 13 Oct. 1954, 1238.

Portier-Young, Anathea E. "Languages of Identity and Obligation: Daniel as Bilingual Book." *Vetus Testamentum* 60 (2010) 98–115.

Rad, Gerhard von. *Old Testament Theology*. Vol. 2: *The Theology of Israel's Prophetic Traditions*. Translated by D. M. G. Stalker. New York: Harper, 1965.

Schwartz, Regina M. *Sacramental Poetics at the Dawn of Secularism: When God Left the World*. Stanford: Stanford University Press, 2008.

Smith, Walter C. "Immortal, Invisible, God only Wise." In *Glory to God: The Presbyterian Hymnal*, 122. Louisville: Westminster John Knox, 2013.

Spina, Frank. "Israelites as Gerim: 'Sojourners' in Historical and Sociological Perspective." In *The Word of the Lord Shall Go Forth: Essays in Honor of David Noel Freedman in Celebration of his Sixtieth Birthday*, edited by Carol Meyers and Michael O'Connor, 321–35. Winona Lake, IN: Eisenbrauns, 1983.

Stone, Samuel John. "The Church's One Foundation." In *Glory to God: The Presbyterian Hymnal*, 321. Louisville: Westminster John Knox, 2013.

Strawn, Brent D., and Nancy R. Bowen, eds. *A God so Near: Essays on Old Testament Theology in Honor of Patrick D. Miller*. Winona Lake, IN: Eisenbrauns, 2003.

Streett, R. Alan. *Caesar and the Sacrament: Baptism: A Rite of Resistance*. Eugene, OR: Cascade Books, 2017.

Styron, William. *Sophie's Choice*. Toronto: Bantam, 1979.

Sweeney, Marvin A. *I & II Kings*. Old Testament Library. Louisville: Westminster John Knox Press, 2007.

———. *The Twelve Prophets*. 2 vols. Berit Olam. Collegeville, MN: Liturgical, 2000.

Terrien, Samuel L. *The Elusive Presence: Toward a New Biblical Theology*. 1978. Reprint, Eugene, OR: Wipf & Stock, 2000.

Trible, Phyllis. *God and the Rhetoric of Sexuality*. Overtures to Biblical Theology. Philadelphia: Fortress, 1978.

Walzer, Michael. *Exodus and Revolution*. New York: Basic Books, 1985.

Watts, Isaac. "O God Our Help in Ages Past." In *The New Century Hymnal*, 25. Cleveland: Pilgrim, 1995.

Weems, Renita J. *Battered Love: Marriage, Sex, and Violence in the Hebrew Prophets*. Overtures to Biblical Theology. Minneapolis: Fortress, 1995.

White, James Boyd. *Living Speech: Resisting the Empire of Force*. Princeton: Princeton University Press, 2006.

Wolterstorff, Nicholas. *Justice in Love*. Grand Rapids: Eerdmans, 2011.

Scripture Index

OLD TESTAMENT

Genesis

	76
1:28–31	61
2	48
2:1–4	61
2:7	47, 48
3	66, 68
12:1	13
15:18–20	13
17:8	13
26:4	13
43:32	76
46:33–34	76
47:13–25	57, 77

Exodus

	23, 36–37, 76
1:8–14	77
2:23–25	30
2:23	23, 84
3:7–9	30, 137
3:10	30, 137
3:11—4:17	30
4:22	56, 77
5:1	30
6:6–8	7
8:26	76
12:26–27	50
12:38	77
13:8	50
15:1–18	31
15:20–21	31, 56
16–18	56
19–24	31, 37, 65–66
19	56
19:5–6	78
19:5	56
19:8	56
19:12	36
19:16–25	133
20:1–17	31, 36, 56
20:1	56, 64
20:2–6	66
20:3–6	163
20:8–17	59
20:13–17	67
20:13–16	59
20:17	59, 167
23:3	25
24:4	56
24:7	56, 159
25–31	37
32–34	5, 37, 63, 66
32	65–68, 150
32:7–9	66
32:10	67
32:11–14	17
32:11–13	6
32:28	5
33:12–23	71
33:19	73
33:21–23	133
34	74
34:6–7	4, 18, 73–74
34:8–9	71
34:10	5

Exodus (continued)

34:20–25	18
35–40	37
40:34–38	37

Leviticus

36–37, 39, 71, 77–78, 165, 168–69, 171

18	165
19	39, 165–66, 168–69
19:2	35–36, 165, 168
19:10	167
19:15	167
19:18	59, 166–67, 168
19:19	165–66
19:34	168
20	165
20:24–26	38
21:8	38
26	13

Numbers

14:13–19	6, 18

Deuteronomy

78, 147, 149, 160–64, 168, 171

1:5	160
4:7	91
5:3	149, 160
5:6–10	163
6	59
6:5	161
6:20–24	58
6:10–11	163
7:5	164
8:12–13	163
8:17–18	163
10:18	162
10:19	162
12–25	161
14:1–2	78
14:3–21	78
15:1–18	161
15:7	161

23	80
23:3–6	78–79
23:19–20	161
24:10–15	162
24:17–22	147, 162
28	13
30:3	161
30:9	163

Joshua

6:1	13
8:1	13
10:8	13
10:19–20	5
10:32	5

Judges

5	20
5:11	21

1 Samuel

1:1	144
6:20	36
16:1–2	136

2 Samuel

6:6–7	36
7:1–16	146
8:15–18	20
11	68
12:9–10	68

1 Kings

4:1–6	20
4:7–19	20
12:1–19	20
18:27	95
18:38–39	133
19:1–18	132
19:5	132
19:11–12	132, 134
19:11	133
19:12	137

Scripture Index

19:13	132, 135	8	47
19:14	135, 137	10	21, 60
19:15	136	10:2–3	21
19:17	136	10:2	21
19:18	137	10:3–4	60
21	22	10:4	21
21:20–24	22	10:5	221
		10:6	21
		10:7–10	60
		10:7	21

2 Kings

4:1–7	22	10:8	21
18:17–36	106	10:9	22
18:26	107	10:10–11	60
18:27–28	107	10:11	21
19:6–7	107	10:12	22
19:21–28	107	10:13	22
19:35–37	107	10:14	22
23:36—24:7	146	10:15	22
24:8–12	146	10:17–18	22
		10:23	21
		22:6	94

2 Chronicles

		22:22	50
36:22–23	78	22:25	50
		23	126
		35:18	50

Ezra

		44:9–14	8
9:1–2	79	47:1	93
9:2	166	51:4–5	70
9:3	79	51:10–12	70
		73	53, 60

Nehemiah

		73:2	53
		73:6	60
8:8	164	73:8	60
13:23–27	79	73:11	60
		73:18–20	53

Job

		73:18	53
		73:24	54
7:17–21	47	73:26	54
31:35–37	122	73:28	54
38–41	122	82	24
38:1	136	82:3–4	24
42:7–8	63	82:5	24
		82:6–7	24

Psalms

		82:8	24
		86	103
	14, 18, 45, 51–53	86:15–17	73
1:2–3	49	88	115n
1:2	51		

Psalms *(continued)*

88:3–4	119
88:5	119
88:6–8a	8–9, 121
88:9	114
88:10–12	120
88:15	120
88:16–18	8–9
88:16	121
88:18	121
96:10	155
98:8	93
100:1	93
103	74
103:4	48
103:8–10	73
103:8	48
103:11	48
103:17	48
103:13–14	48
104:29–30	47
107:32	50
115:4–8	10
119:44–45	63
119:49	51
119:50	51
119:74	51
119:81	51
119:113	63
119:114	51
119:174	63
137	78
139	45, 47
139:1–5	46, 47
139:7–12	47
139:7–11	46
139:13–18	47
139:13–17	46
139:18	46
139:22	14
145–150	48
146:7b–9	8
147:2–6	48
147:8–11	49
147:12–19	49
149:1	50

Proverbs

14:11	167

Isaiah

	96, 98–99, 103
1	96
1:13–15	96
5:8–12	23
6	37
6:2–3	36
6:5	36
13–23	154
42:14–16	7
42:14	95, 101
43:3	72
45:7	11
46:11	155
49:14	99
49:15	99
54:1	98
54:4–6	98
54:7–8	97, 99
55:1–2	128
56	80
56:4–5	80
56:6–7a	80–81
61:3–4	74
65:24	114

Jeremiah

1:4–10	143
1:10	144, 149
2:3	143
3:1–5	14
3:2	143
3:19–20	14
4:19–20	143
4:23–26	143
5	32
5:12	9, 60
5:26–28	32
7:1–15	143–48
7:1–2	144
7:3	144
7:4	144

7:5–7	144	31:33	74
7:7	144	31:34	98
7:8–11	144	32:38	151
7:12–15	144	32:40–41	151
7:15	145	32:44	150
7:16–34	144	33:7	161
6:13–15	23	33:11	150, 161
9:23–24	23	33:20–21	151
10:16	156	33:25–26	151
11:2	149	33:26	150, 161
11:4	149, 150	36:22–32	98
15:5–10	6	38:4	147
22:8–9	149	46–51	13, 154
22:13–14	146	46	154
22:15–16	33	47–49	154
22:18–19	146	50–51	154
22:28–30	146	50:2	154
23:1–2	146	50:8–10	154
23:9–22	146	50:18	154
23:23	91	50:31–32	154
23:24	91	51:1–5	154
25:9	153	51:15–16	156
26	147	51:19	156
26:1–19	146–48	51:59–64	153–57
26:1–6	147	51:64	154–55
26:7–10	147		
26:10–11	147	## Lamentations	
26:12–13	147		
26:14	147	5:20	99
26:15	147		
26:16–19	147	## Ezekiel	
26:18	147		
26:24	146–48		125
27–28	148	16:14–15	6
27:6	153	16:35–43	5
28:14	149, 150	22:26	38–39
29–33	149	25–32	154
29:3–9	149	34	127
29:14	150, 161	34:1–10	146
30–31	150, 153, 155	34:11–16a	127
30:2	149	34:16b	127
30:3	161	36:22–32	98
30:17	150	36:26–27	74
30:22	150	47:13—48:29	125
31:8–9	156		
21:11–12	156	## Daniel	
31:20	151		
31:31–34	149–52	1	170

Daniel (continued)

1:3–4	108
1:4	108
1:6–7	107
2:47	108
3:29	108
4:27	109
4:37	108
6:26–27	108–9

Hosea

2	74
2:2–13	73
2:12–13	5
2:14–15	73
3:1	5
4:1	67
4:2	67

Amos

	23
1–2	13, 154
1:3	13
1:6	13
1:9	13
1:11	13
1:13	13
4:6–11	5
6:4–6	23
8:4–6	61

Micah

2:1–2	23
3:9	23
3:12	147

Habakkuk

	117
2:6–19	87, 90
2:6	87, 88
2:9	87, 88
2:12	87, 88
2:15	87, 88
2:18–19	90, 93, 94
2:19	87, 88
2:20	87, 88, 90, 129, 130
3	90
3:1–19	90
3:1–16	88, 89
3:2	89
3:3ff.	89
3:3–15	89, 133
3:13–15	94
3:13	88
3:14	89
3:15	89
3:16–19	87
3:16	89
3:17–19	88
3:17	89
3:19	89

Zephaniah

1:7	91
1:12	9, 60

~

NEW TESTAMENT

Matthew

2:23–34	168
5:21	63
5:44	168
5:48	168
11:7–9	135
11:30	33
17:24	20
22:17–19	20
22:40	159
25:40	167–68

Mark

	81
6:30–44	82
7	82
7:1–23	81, 165

Scripture Index

7:24–30	81	21:39	109
7:26–29	39	21:40	105, 110, 128
7:28	112	22:1–21	111
10:45	72	22:2	110
12:28–34	159	22:3–21	110
12:32–33	59	22:3	110
12:37	26	22:4	110
		22:6	110
		22:8	111

Luke

		22:21	110, 111
1:52–53	25	22:22–29	106
2:1–5	20	22:22–23	111
5:27	32	22:22	105, 110–11
7:22	25, 32	22:29	105
9:59	32		
15:17	54		
18:22	32		

Romans

18:28—19:16	148	2:11	25
19:47–48	32	4:17	6
20:21	25	8:19–23	103
23:21	105	9–11	39
		10:11–13	40
		11:2–3	139
		11:5	139

John

10:16	112	12:2	159
18:28—19:16	148	13:6–7	20

Acts

1 Corinthians

5:37	20	12:25	152
9	112		

Galatians

10	82, 112		
10:9–16	39		33
10:12	82		
10:14	82	2:6	25
10:15–16	112	3:28	112
10:15	39	4:31—5:1	33
10:28	39	5:1	33
10:34	25, 83, 112	5:14	159–60, 171
21:21	110	5:19–21	170
21:27—22:29	105	5:22–23	170
21:27–36	106	6:2	160, 171
21:28	110		

Ephesians

21:33	105		
21:34	105	4:22–24	40
21:35	105	5:31	40
21:36	105, 110, 111	6:9	25
21:37–40	106		

Colossians

3:2	25
3:12–15	40–41

Philippians

2:4–5	159

Hebrews

8:6	151
8:8–12	151

1 Peter

1:14–16	41

Revelation

	71, 123, 125, 128, 155
6:1—9:21	123
6:1—7:17	124
6:1–17	128
6:8	124
7:1–17	127, 128
7:2	124
7:3	125
7:4–8	125
7:9	126
7:11	126
7:12	126
7:14	125
7:15–17	126
7:16–17	128
7:16	126
7:17	126
8:1	109, 123, 124, 128
8:2—9:21	124
8:3ff.	129
8:13	129
11:15	129
21:3–4	130

Author Index

Adams, Samuel L., 80
Albertz, Rainer, 116
Alexander, Cecil Francis, 159
Anderson, Carol, 103
Augustine, 112

Barth, Karl, 66, 69
Beck, Richard, 37–38, 165
Bishop, Bill, 166
Block, Peter, 162
Bowen, Nancy R., 91
Brueggemann, Walter, 130

Coates, Ta-Nehisi, 84
Coffin, Henry Sloan, 101
Croly, George, 140

Davis, Ellen F., 124
Dear, John, 138
Dempsey, Carol J., 97
Descartes, René, 10, 28, 29
Desmond, Matthew, 162
Douglas, Mary, 166

Endo, Shusaku, 117

Fishbane, Michael, 61–62, 158
Fretheim, Terence E., 119, 137

Gerstenberger, Erhard S., 116
Goodman, Lenn Evan, 165

Janowski, Bernd, 115, 120

Kahl, Brigitte, 33, 169, 171
Kant, Immanuel, 29
King, Martin Luther, Jr., 27, 138

Knohl, Israel, 92

Lapsley, Jacqueline E., 98
Lehmann, Paul, 138
Levenson, Jon D., 58, 62
Lévinas, Emmanuel, 166
Lindström, Fredrik, 121
Locke, John, 28–29
Luther, Martin, 112

Macpherson, C. B., 28–29
McKnight, John, 162
Miller, Patrick D., 61, 91, 164
Moltmann, Jürgen, 139

Niebuhr, Reinhold, 69
Nussbaum, Martha, 169

O'Brien, Julia M., 97
O'Connor, Kathleen M., 96

Paarlberg, Robert, 170
Paton, Alan, 11
Portier-Young, Anathea E., 108

Rad, Gerhard von, 98

Schmitt, Rüdiger, 116
Schwartz, Regina M., 93
Smith, Walter C., 35
Spina, Frank, 168
Stone, Samuel John, 71
Strawn, Brent D., 91
Streett, R. Alan, 160
Styron, William, 122
Sweeney, Marvin A., 92, 134

Author Index

Terrien, Samuel, 133, 135, 138–39
Trible, Phyllis, 99

Walzer, Michael, 23–24, 30
Watts, Isaac, 128

Weems, Renita J., 97
White, James Boyd, 139, 171
Wolterstorff, Nicholas, 166

www.ingramcontent.com/pod-product-compliance
Lightning Source LLC
Chambersburg PA
CBHW020843160426
43192CB00007B/770